Inventing
the Real World

Inventing the Real World

The Art of Alain Robbe-Grillet

Marjorie H. Hellerstein

Selinsgrove: Susquehanna University Press
London: Associated University Presses

© 1998 by Associated University Presses, Inc.

All rights reserved. Authorization to photocopy items for internal or personal use, or the internal or personal use of specific clients, is granted by the copyright owner, provided that a base fee of $10.00, plus eight cents per page, per copy is paid directly to the copyright Clearance Center, 222 Rosewood Drive, Danvers, Massachusetts 01923. [1–57591–010–1/98 $10.00 + 8¢ pp, pc.]

Associated University Presses
440 Forsgate Drive
Cranbury, NJ 08512

Associated University Presses
16 Barter Street
London WC1A 2AH, England

Associated University Presses
P.O. Box 338, Port Credit
Mississauga, Ontario
Canada L5G 4L8

The paper used in this publication meets the requirements
of the American National Standard for Permanence of Paper
for Printed Library Materials Z39.48–1984.

Library of Congress Cataloging-in-Publication Data

Hellerstein, Marjorie H., 1924-
    Inventing the real world : the art of Alain Robbe-Grillet / Marjorie H. Hellerstein.
    p.   cm.
    Includes bibliographical references and index.
    ISBN 1-57591-010-1 (alk. paper)
    1. Robbe-Grillet, Alain, 1922- —Film and video adaptations. 2. Motion pictures and literature. I. Title.
    PQ2635.0117Z65   1998
    791.43'6--dc20   97–20753
                                                                                                                                       CIP

PRINTED IN THE UNITED STATES OF AMERICA

Contents

Introduction: Reality and Truth in Modern Fiction	9
1. Origins and Attitudes: Robbe-Grillet States His Beliefs	21
2. Confused and Misled: The Narrator Takes Part in an Old Myth	35
3. The Hidden *I* and the Camera Eye: Novels and a Film Re-Create Obsession	59
4. Perception and Deception: *The Man Who Lies* and *Djinn*	80
5. Vision, Visualization, and Interpenetration	102
6. Author? Author	133
Notes	140
Film Glossary	148
Bibliography	157
Index	169

Inventing
the Real World

Introduction:
Reality and Truth in Modern Fiction

The novel has always encouraged a belief in its realism, and in the nineteenth and twentieth centuries that belief has been a preoccupation with both writers and theorists. In *Mimesis: The Representation of Reality in Western Literature*, Erich Auerbach chose Flaubert as a leader in the movement toward modern realism. Auerbach defined modern realism as "the serious treatment of everyday reality" and "the embedding of random persons and events in the general course of contemporary history."[1] Flaubert's role in the movement, that is, in the nineteenth-century inception of the movement, was his use of language. It was the basis of his artistic practice and was derived from his "profound faith in the truth of language, responsibly, candidly, and carefully employed . . . [and his belief] that the truth of the phenomenal world is also revealed in linguistic expression" (486).

Auerbach assumed, and most of his readers assumed, that the phenomenal world is the real world, and representing the real world in fiction requires that it be observed very closely. Observation is done by a particular self, and that self is unique. As Flaubert said, "Is not everything an illusion? . . . Our way of perceiving objects" is all the truth there is.[2] A kind of truth is Flaubert's goal, through perception, observation, transformation, using language carefully—all by "our way."

"Our way" clearly indicates that the real world is not a fixed world, and many twentieth-century philosophers have agreed with that view, emphasizing its importance for artists, who "must rid themselves of the burden of knowledge in their efforts to portray the world precisely as they see it."[3] The artist may be precise in his/her observations, or he/she may deliberately distort those observations, but, according to phenomenologists, the artist fosters a relationship to the world based on perception and then uses the relationship to "know" the world. "[W]e find in perception," said the phenomenologist Maurice Merleau-Ponty, "a mode of access to the object that is rediscovered at every level."[4] Perception, for Merleau-Ponty, stands for the whole experience of making a relationship between the self and the external world, the world of objects. "[T]o perceive," said Merleau-Ponty, "is to render oneself present to something through the body" (42).

In phenomenological thinking, the self sees, experiences, and organizes the world in its own way; the self is always idiosyncratic in its seeing and organizing because it cannot help but do its own work through its own body. In the practice of fictional realism, representation becomes a matter of presentation of the self's unique perceptions; as an artist, the self expresses its environment by structuring it in a particular way.

The critic Stephen Heath believes that Robbe-Grillet does not have phenomenological insight. Robbe-Grillet believes, he says, in a "passive reality of the world," whereas phenomenological perception wishes to restructure existence.[5] In Heath's reading of Robbe-Grillet's 1958 essay "Nature, Humanism, and Tragedy," published in *For a New Novel* in 1965, Robbe-Grillet is primarily concerned with the "cleansing power of vision": "If everything is visible in itself under the inspection of the eye able to recognize in this inspection the absolute and necessary separation between individual and world of things, then the problem of otherness ... will disappear" (108). In Heath's reading of the essay, Robbe-Grillet removes meaning by this means, leaving only what is to be seen (as "scene") and accepted. Because of his essay, Heath says, Robbe-Grillet leaves himself open to attacks as a moving spirit in the *chosiste* (thingness) school and the *regard* (look/eye) school. These may be false interpretations, Heath says, but Robbe-Grillet asked for it.

What does Robbe-Grillet say in "Nature, Humanism, and Tragedy"?[6] He begins with an epigram from Roland Barthes that rejects tragedy as an insidious means of "recovering" human misery, of justifying it as a form of wisdom and purification, a way of thinking that Barthes believes must be fought and that Robbe-Grillet proceeds to fight. Tragedy establishes its hold over humankind by projecting anthropomorphic qualities onto things and nature and thus producing an "anthropocentric atmosphere," obliquely significant and sentimental. Man is connected to things and nature by analogy, that is by anthropomorphising metaphors. Endowing nature or objects with human emotions produces, Robbe-Grillet thinks, a form of predestination for human beings that is negative. This is traditional humanism, he says, and must be rejected in the name of man's freedom. Man is man and things are things, used by man but not implying a common or higher nature for these two separate entities. "For if he [man] rejects communion, he rejects tragedy" (59).

Firmly separating man and things, primarily by the use of description through sight, is Robbe-Grillet's stated goal. "To limit oneself to description [without analogy] is obviously to reject all the other modes of approaching the object: sympathy as unrealistic, tragedy as alienating, comprehension as answerable to the realm of science exclusively" (70). Through description, "the cleansing power of the sense of sight . . . leaves things in their respective place" (73). This power, he says, was "acknowledged" by Sartre in some of his descriptions in *Nausea* and remains a good tool, "especially if it keeps exclusively to outlines." Man is *one*, not doubled, and "things," once "scoured clean" (74), refer only to themselves. *Meaning* is removed from things for the sake of man—to free him from the sense of tragedy. Man's point of view does the seeing, without *predestined* signification.

Does this mean that Robbe-Grillet's way of thinking is quite different from phenomenological thinking and that his writing has no connection to phenomenological thinking? The critic John Sturrock has a contrary view. He thinks that the whole Nouveau Roman (new novel) genre is a concrete expression of the philosophy of phenomenology: it is reflective and interrogative and exposes the process of composition in response to the way our image of the world is changed; it does not attempt to imitate reality but takes place in the consciousness of the novelist and thus continues the narrative tradition of the interior monologue; in it, time is used to portray the succession of mental experiences of the self; *things* are emphasized because there is a consciousness to see them.[7] In addition, the new novelist and his/her readers understand that the novel is a fabrication and that the novelist is only a man/woman with his own viewpoint on the world, from which he cannot escape. Readers construct the work by understanding it, solving it, though the puzzle is rarely definable (34). Readers who understand the phenomenological mode of narration will learn how to identify with the act of writing itself and even with the process of living (36).[8]

Another important critic of Robbe-Grillet's work, Bruce Morrissette, insists on the role of the reader in recognizing and reawakening to the forms that Robbe-Grillet uses:

> [T]he reader or spectator must "decondition" himself, become free to see things with a fresh vision; the novelist and scenarist as well must cultivate a *creative formalism* based on the principle that both novel and film exist as art. The values of art are never ideological, sociological, or political; they reside only in forms and structures.[9]

Morrissette's analyses of Robbe-Grillet's forms and structures have revealed a number of persistently recurring techniques: restructured chronology; metamorphoses; duplications of themes, characters, events, verbal enigmas, and mythic allusions; double meanings of words; and the use of a major ellipse or hole in the narrated action.

As is true in the understanding of any form of art, an awareness of techniques and devices is necessary and valuable. However, because of the place of this fiction in the history of fiction, awareness of technique is not enough to illuminate the purposes of this form of writing. The techniques do serve to underscore how separate from the real world is this fiction, how much the work and its world as created in Robbe-Grillet's fiction are independent from the real world, how the author "manipulates" the real world, as Jean Alter said, to suit his will.[10]

Alain Robbe-Grillet is well aware of the difficulties of defining his ideas and his work as well as the ideas and practices of the novelists with whom he has been associated.

The French New Novel was never a school, even less a comprehensive literary theory. Its very existence as a group of writers has always been questioned, often first by those considered as the main representatives of the movement. Ask Butor, Pinget, Duras, Simon, Ollier, Sarraute if their work belongs to the New Novel. None will admit it without reservation and several would fiercely and wholly oppose such a classification.[11]

The independence and freedom of invention of these writers prevents their agreement on a way of writing, an adherence to common conventions. They are all different, Robbe-Grillet says, but they do share a "creative passion . . . the necessity of new forms, open and free . . . their refusal to accept the narrative conventions of the nineteenth century . . . (and) immutable laws" (201).

Nevertheless, Robbe-Grillet does give a "provisional" definition of the New Novel and its practitioners based on their perceptions of the world:

[It] is closer to what we know today about man and his world, carefully describing discontinuous and fragile fragments, the misleading combinations of which seem always to be searching for possible meaning, which then sketches itself out, but at the same time escapes, crumbles, and soon takes a new shape, again provisional. (202)

Provisional and paradoxical the New Novel may be, but it has not been invited to join the ranks of the newest novels, now called postmodern. Donald Barthelme, an approved postmodernist, has called the new novel genre "leaden, self-conscious in the wrong way. Painfully slow-paced, with no loops of the imagination, concentrating on the minutiae of consciousness."[12]

Whatever the right way of self-consciousness is, the critic Terry Eagleton has, in turn, called postmodern culture "depthless, styleless, dehistoricized, decathected surfaces . . . [in which] authenticity is quite unintelligible."[13]

Perhaps the New Novel is lucky to escape the label of postmodern. Frederic Jameson also considers postmodernist culture to be dehistoricized and dehistoricizing, and he notes that the concept is "not merely contested, it is also internally conflicted and contradictory."[14] Jameson discusses the work of some Nouveau Roman writers in his book *Postmodernism or The Cultural Logic of Late Capitalism* but seems unable to determine whether the Nouveau Roman belongs to late-flowering high modernism or to postmodernism. He further notes that his interest in postmodernism has led to an accusation that he has betrayed his Marxist connections. It seems to be dangerous to be too closely identified with a movement, a theory, a revolution in creativity, and it is not the purpose of this study to associate Robbe-Grillet too closely with any group but rather to read his works as he wrote them, following his descriptive method wherever it goes, adapting to its complexities. As the critic Victor Shklovsky says in discussing the method of describing precisely. "[It creates] a special perception of the object—it creates a 'vision' of the object instead of serving as a means for knowing it."[15] Creating a vision of the object by concentrating on minutiae changes the object, enlarges or diminishes it, and connects it to its context without defining its significance; the narrative voice becomes dominant and demands the attention of the readers, without satisfying their expectations. The reader-author connection that Robbe-Grillet hopes to effect is similar to the reading process discussed in Wolfgang Iser's essay "The reading process: a phenomenological approach."[16] Iser says that the reader uses the text, with its perspectives and patterns, to set the work in motion in order that it can awaken responses within him/her self. Only when the reading is active and creative will it give pleasure; from the pleasure, helped by the reader's imagination, the unwritten implications of the text give its situations far greater significance than they might have seemed to have.

> The fact that completely different readers can be differently affected by texts transforms reading into a creative process that is far above mere perception of what is written. The literary text activates our own faculties, enabling us to recreate the world it presents. . . . [This is] the virtual dimension of the text. . . . This virtual dimension is . . . the coming together of text and imagination. (215)

INTRODUCTION 15

Robbe-Grillet Speaks for Himself

In the catalogue of the paintings of Mark Tansey, published in 1993, the painting entitled *Robbe-Grillet Cleansing Every Object in Sight* is discussed by the organizer of the exhibition as a significant statement of Tansey's beliefs about art imagery:

> Tansey believes that every image can yield meaning if the viewer makes the effort multisensorily. *Robbe-Grillet Cleansing Every Object in Sight*, 1981 (cat. No. 3), depicts the French author and filmmaker Alain Robbe-Grillet in what appears to be a desert, scrubbing stones, which on close view reveal themselves to be, not stone, but monumental miniatures—Stonehenge, the Matterhorn, the Sphinx, the monoliths of Monument Valley—as well as elemental volumes and assorted cultural icons, each representing general aspects of civilization. Through his determined scrubbing, Robbe-Grillet attempts to strip these stones of their content, no doubt a reference to his wish to remove hidden meanings from every object.[17]

The last statement cites *For a New Novel* (1963) as the source for the idea that Robbe-Grillet is determined to remove meaning from objects. As has been noted in this introduction, ascribing meanings to things, that is, by creating metaphoric connections between things and human beings for the sake of emotional and sentimental excitation, was once rejected by Robbe-Grillet. He has since parodied rather than rejected the metaphoric process, as he has created ambiguous, unresolved situations and chance-inspired paradoxes for his narrative consciousnesses.

Robbe-Grillet's comments on the Tansey painting appear in two places: in *Ghosts in the Mirror* (*Le miroir qui revient*), his autobiography/novel (or, romanesque), and in the catalogue of the Tansey exhibition. In *Ghosts in the Mirror*, his statement is appreciative of the painting's humor:

> I recognize myself in this very witty allegory with pleasure. But having carefully cleaned the pieces, am I not now artfully putting them in order? Perhaps even sticking them together again to shape a destiny, a statue, the little boy's terrors and joys forming a solid base for the themes or techniques of the future writer.[18]

Several revelations about Robbe-Grillet's purposes are suggested in this statement: his reordering of past images and artifacts for an "artful" purpose, his belief in a basis of subconscious "terrors and joys" from the writer's past that account for what is in his work, and the presence of "themes" in a writer's (his) work. He does not quite agree with Tansey's interpretation.

In the Mark Tansey catalogue, his response to the painting is through the creation of an imaginative work, a work that may raise questions about how he "rejects" meanings, historical symbols, cultural icons. The story in the catalogue is called "A Graveyard of Identities and Uniforms." The story's central character is Henri de Corinthe, a paradoxical figure from Robbe-Grillet's past, possibly real, certainly for his purposes fictionalized and made mythic, who appears in Robbe-Grillet's last three works, published in 1984, 1988, and 1994.[19] He has called these works "romanesques," implying that they are forms of novels—but he clearly talks about himself in these "fictions." The first paragraph of the story in the catalogue introduces elements of uncertainty and humor:

> We are now in the depths of a very hard winter of indeterminate date. ... He wears the glorious black uniform of a member of the crack cavalry school at Saumur, of which he was not long ago instructing officer. He appears to be lost, at least in thought.[20]

The figure rides on a white horse into what was formerly a large market town, now destroyed by bombardments and conflagration. A precise description of the area, geometric and diagrammatic, is given, and then a horse and man are discovered, the horse (black) bending over a young German lieutenant with no apparent wound but lifeless. Henri de Corinthe and the German lieutenant have the same last name and identical photographs on their identity cards. A photograph of a young woman, Marie-Ange (who also has appeared in Robbe-Grillet's romanesques), is discovered. She is naked and being menaced by a rifle. As the (second?) black horse follows de Corinthe out of town, he thinks this might be a "monumental graveyard, shelled by mistake," and he notices "in the foreground, toward the lower right hand corner of the frame" (has the scene now become a painting?) a "stone . . .

[that] still exhibits the name of the builder of mausoleums and cenotaphs: Mark Tansey, Architect" (11).

The joke is now on Tansey. Is Tansey's art—the use of real events and real (borrowed) photographs and paintings—a form of memorialization, of tomb-building? Is Tansey using pre-used objects to create meaning or to confuse meaning? Robbe-Grillet permits himself to question Tansey's purposes with tongue in cheek. Indeed, all of Robbe-Grillet's work has a mock solemnity and irony that transcends much postmodern irony; that is, it points beyond cynicism and mockery to an attitude about the paradoxical nature of events.

Both Tansey and Robbe-Grillet construct forms, using their freedom as artists to create by borrowing, inventing, re-visioning, re-presenting. Robbe-Grillet's humor and his refusal of faith and engagement may imply a rejection of any meaning, but in fact he accepts the complexity of life, which he defines as "fragmentary, fleeting, useless, so accidental and so specific that any incident at any moment appears gratuitous and any life seems in the end devoid of the slightest unifying signification."[21] Meaning exists in life in confusing abundance, but a unified explanation of the meaning of life—real or fictional—is elusive.

> The advent of the modern novel is precisely linked to this discovery: reality is discontinuous, composed of elements juxtaposed at random, each of them unique and all the more difficult to grasp in that they emerge in an always unforeseen, irrelevant, haphazard way. (160)

This way of thinking is opposed to what he calls "realist ideology," which sees the world as closed, rigid, full of meaning, linear, following laws of reason, with characters that become types, until Flaubert helped develop another "family" of novelists: "those who will explore, going further with each decade, insoluble tensions, ruptures, narrative aporias, fractures, voids, etc., because they know that reality begins at the precise moment when meaning becomes uncertain" (163).

As Robbe-Grillet sees Flaubert, that writer did more than observe the world carefully. He revealed the uncertainty of knowing what his observation meant. Nevertheless, though the world eludes definition and shows no clear direction of intention, Robbe-

Grillet recognizes his own compulsions. As he says in *Ghosts in the Mirror*, writing for him is a necessary pursuit, from within himself, speaking of himself, pursued in order to "exorcise the ghosts I couldn't come to terms with . . . to destroy, by describing them exactly, the nocturnal monsters that threaten to invade my waking life" (11). His meanings are "devious," but he will not succumb to the "fatal temptation to take annihilation for ultimate bliss, loss of consciousness for illumination, despair for beauty of soul" as the war and its terrible consequences might have encouraged him to feel (27).

His refusal of faith comes from a conviction that there is too much faithlessness, against which he defends himself by humor, expressed through inversions of myths, puns, ironic circles of action, doubled central figures, and lies—all part of the storytelling of each of his stories.

He is also rejecting the expected forms of narrative—continuity, linear chronology, causality, noncontradiction—by his use of "complicated sequences, digressions, cuts and repetitions, aporias, blind alleys, shifts in perspective, various permutations, dislocations or inversions, etc. (21). His complicated purposes—against hope, against smug certainties of past literature—along with the inescapable impressions and emotions of the real world, have produced in his writing images that are startlingly like the images produced by hallucinations. Although hallucinations are individual and internal, the researcher Ronald Siegel has noted that they all have much in common. They are "all characterized by excitation and the production of images from memory and imagination." Many of them use basic geometric forms, particularly a "lattice-tunnel form," which are often succeeded by complex images from "childhood memories and scenes associated with strong emotional experiences.[22]

Many of Robbe-Grillet's repetitions and blind alleys appear in his novels and his films as mazes, labyrinths, circular routes. These routes and passages help structure his work, help acclimate the reader to the reading process. And, as Robbe-Grillet reveals in his autobiography, childhood memories and strong emotional experiences are sources for the strong impressions that he attempts to describe in order to challenge the superficial certainties of the world.

As Siegel says, "Like a mirage that shows a magnificent city, the images of hallucinations are actually reflected images of real objects located elsewhere" (116).

Robbe-Grillet creates his labyrinthine spaces, his overly precise objects, with an illusion of language that re-creates hallucinatory states. Hallucinations are often an attempt by the mind to escape the world, even though they can themselves be terrifying. Robbe-Grillet's "mirages" are products of his escape to freedom, his playing with images, ideas, myths, accepted beliefs, not just for the sake of form but as a challenge to himself and to the reader to experience complex forms of narrative and complex reactions to experience.

The Purpose of This Study

Robbe-Grillet is known as an audacious experimenter, a breaker of tradition, a revolutionary of consciousness, and each of his works attests to a restless imagination seeking unique outlets. Each work he produces is a new creation in the sense that each new work demands a new approach to narrative diegesis and to the source and organization of the material for fiction; each reflects a different stage of his creative purposes. In "On the Phenomenology of the Creative Process," Georg Lukacs defines a creative process and its creative result as inevitable because of the way a "genius" creator functions:

> [T]he creator is a genius if his experiences contain the technical forms of the work as necessary experiential forms, if for him the relationships which constitute the work are the relationships of his immediate experience; the man who experiences *subspecie formae*, for whom the technique of the work is the natural communicative form.[23]

Considered by this standard, Robbe-Grillet's experiments in form and effect must be understood as inextricably bound to their sources; his work necessarily contains his experiences (in the phenomenological sense), and his experiences are communicated by whatever technique is "natural" for his communication. As he subverts the usual expectations of literary creation or of film creation, he is using the experiences of his relationship with past forms of those arts and creating new relationships.

As an artist, Robbe-Grillet uses his mediums—language and the moving image—in ways that are suggested by the mediums themselves. Language (as *parole*, *langue*, *langage*, in contemporary critical terminology) is manipulable in an extraordinary number of ways: through individual words, collections of words in phrases and sentences, arrangements of paragraphs, recurrences of rhythms, meanings deriving from language, meanings confused by language. Film, as has always been true in the history of the medium, is dependent on its techniques. In any definition of *artist*, the imaginative and knowledgeable use of the raw material of each art form is an essential part of its meaning.

Robbe-Grillet's relationships to old and contemporary myths, to women, and to ideologies are integral to his works, and his process as a creator can best be understood by close description of several works (as will be done in this study) and by a reconstruction of his connections to contemporary life, as revealed in recurrent themes, motifs, and techniques. Perhaps these patterns and persistent images also reveal Robbe-Grillet's secret motives and desires, and readers are free to speculate as they choose.

It is hoped that a highly conscious reading/seeing of Robbe-Grillet's work will guide his readers/viewers to experience his works for their appeals to humankind's need for ludic challenges and for their beauties of language rhythms, of images, and of organization and entwined connections—all for the sake of encouraging intellectual and aesthetic absorption in literature as art.[24]

1
Origins and Attitudes: Robbe-Grillet States His Beliefs

In 1953, after he had achieved a certain fame, primarily because of *The Voyeur* and *Last Year at Marienbad*, Alain Robbe-Grillet published a collection of essays, some previously published, some not before published, called *For a New Novel* (*Pour un nouveau roman*). The title declared that he was ready to make a manifesto, a proposal and a challenge for the future of the novel. He did not see himself as an eccentric, isolated practitioner of the art of the novel but as part of its evolution. In the twentieth century, others had already created works that were breaks with the past and moves toward the future. In the section "Elements of a Modern Anthology," Robbe-Grillet discussed five such writers, not necessarily the most important and not necessarily his favorite, but writers who would serve as examples

> which will permit me to focus on certain themes and characteristic forms of this literature still in progress. The earliest of these examples already date back some fifty years, the latest belong to our own postwar period. All of them offer, from my point of view, something profoundly immediate; it is that *something* which I am trying to isolate here, and which it would not be difficult to recognize in most contemporary explorations.[1]

Robbe-Grillet's first example is Raymond Roussel (1877–1933), a writer who, Robbe-Grillet says, "[has] nothing to say, and [he] says it badly." Yet Roussel is "one of the direct ancestors of the modern novel." It is his extraordinary ability to create a particular kind of universe, according to Robbe-Grillet, that makes him a progenitor of the modern novel. His universe is "*flat* and *discontinuous* . . . where each thing refers only to itself."[2] In spite of the enlargement of details, the enigmas and complex mysteries that make up Roussel's plots and themes, and the numerous unexplained symbolic-like events and objects, Roussel's universe is deliberately obvious, trite, and without significance. There is no higher meaning in the symbols and mysteries. Everything "meaningful" is solved and explained by Roussel in a very simplified way.

Robbe-Grillet is attracted to Roussel's ability to create a universe that is difficult to relate to real life, that begins and ends in the book itself (even stylistically, his opening and closing sentences *sound* identical, though the words in each sentence have different meanings), and that treats time as a series of immediate moments "in movement, but frozen in the middle of movement" (86).

Another writer who creates a universe separate from the real world and exclusively from within the mind of his protagonist is Italo Svevo (1861–1928). In the essay called "Zeno's Sick Conscience," Robbe-Grillet describes the protagonist's acute self-awareness, self-consciousness, and self-hate. Such a mental universe, he notes, changes the protagonist's feelings about what is "natural" in life. What is natural for him is sickness and a nurturing of the feelings of sickness. His persistent concern with sickness results in an inability to separate his actions and thoughts into discrete time units, to use language to speak the truth, or to act without being conscious of every action. Zeno, for Robbe-Grillet, represents the condition of man as no longer "innocent," that is, man who is unable to act without thinking about his act. The condition of art parallels that of man: "the style of a novel, in its turn, can no longer be innocent."[3] The mind of the novelist and the style of the novel are central concerns in his art, matching the protagonist's mental universe. The style and the mental universe are both self-absorbed and highly conscious of their forms and structures. Italo Svevo has caught a modern condition of man and a necessary form for a modern novel.

1 / ORIGINS AND ATTITUDES

Another novelist in Robbe-Grillet's anthology of models for the new novelist is Joë Bousquet (1897?–1950).[4] Bousquet's paralysis from a war wound literally confined him in space and in his experiences in the real world. His experiences became those of memory and of dream, and they absorbed his attention completely. He was not distracted by physical action or by a need to verify the actuality of what he imagined. He was free to create and live within a completely imaginative universe and to give that universe sensual reality. For Robbe-Grillet, Joë Bousquet pointed the way for the dream to become a model for the kind of reality art should create, with the inventiveness as well as the clarity and precision of dream images. Only a free and active imagination unhampered by the need to imitate the forms and relationships of the real world can truly invent a new universe, the only universe that the novelist of the new consciousness should consider.

Since Robbe-Grillet has stated that the only reality that makes sense as a creation is an invented reality and that such invented reality must immediately engulf its readers or audiences, he responds to art that presents any reality as immediate. Samuel Beckett (1906–93) created plays and characters in that condition of being, or *being there* (in the Heideggerian sense). Everything that happens to the characters (or does not happen to them) is governed by only one fact: they are before us on the stage. They are *present*. Their presence finally impresses us, not their past or their future. Presence stands for the human condition, without making a judgment as to whether this condition is desirable or not. A direct impression of being there, of presence, of immediacy, is related to man's consciousness of life. *Presence as consciousness of life* expresses Robbe-Grillet's belief that fiction, in order to be related to life, does not have to represent significant ideas:

> [T]he universe thus defined is necessarily deprived of sense in the two acceptations of the term in French: it excludes any idea of *direction* (seen) as well as any *signification* (sens).[5]

Though Beckett's universe would seem to be static—without direction, without meaning—it nevertheless has an internal rhythm and movement. The style has managed to make the audience feel this, and style again is important in the works of Robert

Pinget (1919–). He has a style that creates a sense of constant movement; everything is in the process of being made as the novel proceeds, particularly the characters. "They are *pure creations* which derive only from the spirit of creation.[6] In the same way, Robbe-Grillet says, the story is in a constant state of invention, changing, turning in circles, unexpectedly becoming cohesive. Both the characters and the fictions that they constantly make up about themselves and about each other "turn against the reality from which they had emerged" (129). Constant invention and surprise change the reality. Pinget's protagonists are often artists (writers and painters), and they are the makers of the scenes in which they take part. Protagonist and narrator merge in Pinget's work. For Robbe-Grillet, such an elusive narrator, who takes shape in more than one protagonist, is the answer to the omniscient narrators of the nineteenth-century novels.

All the novelists discussed by Robbe-Grillet create a fictional reality that is different from external reality, either because their protagonists have peculiar mental or physical universes or because the style of their books dominates the events: scenes change and move because the images and sentence rhythms must change and move in order to satisfy certain patterns of imagination. "[Style] constitutes reality,"[7] and description makes style. Robbe-Grillet's stories are described instead of told, and his descriptions reveal the imaginative transformations, the arrangement and rearrangement of parts, and the mental perspectives that constitute the content of his narratives. Beginning with Flaubert (for modern realism), consciousness of style, on the writer's part and on the reader's part, has been overwhelmingly more important than plot, climax, denouement.

> I do not transcribe, I construct. This had been even the old ambition of Flaubert: to make something out of nothing, something that would stand alone, without having to lean on anything external to the work; today this is the ambition of the novel as a whole. (162)

The "new realism," as Robbe-Grillet calls it in this essay, is identified with a new reality, since "*everything is constantly changing and there is always something new*" (168). The new novelist of realism (the new novelist) is no longer interested in the "lifelike" or the "typical" or in "verisimilitude." In his writing, details are used abundantly, but they are not used to prove the possible existence of such a place or such a character; they are "cut off from signification, hence from their *verisimilitude* . . . not seeming to correspond to any function or precise intention" (163).

Gustave Flaubert and Franz Kafka are important figures in the history of the novel, and they are writers who have prefigured the new direction and meaning (*sens* and *sens*) for the modern novel. Robbe-Grillet has evolved his own theories about the processes of constructing the new realism, sometimes talking about it first, sometimes doing it first, and then reflecting on what he has done in interviews and articles. His "autobiographies" are still another way that he has reflected on (and, in their inventions, has reflected) his methods of creation.

Description, not telling, directs his style, a concept of description that transforms previously accepted forms of description: metaphor, structure, narrative point of view, and movement. His novels and his films are closely related to each other because they all are creatures of his descriptive methods.

Metaphor, Metonymy, and Motif in Robbe-Grillet's Concept of Description

Comparison has been the basis of metaphor-making, comparison between a writer's imagination and a reader's, comparison in the meanings of objects. Metaphors for Robbe-Grillet serve an entirely different function and are made by a different process than comparison. The form of metaphor called metonymy is an integral part of his style and the movement of his style. Metonyms are movements and variations on an original image, the variations connected by parallelism, contradiction, or expansion. The original description may be transformed beyond recognition, but it remains linked to each of its transformations.

Robbe-Grillet's novels and films are alike in that either a point-of-view eye (the camera eye) or an "eye" I, usually not exactly identified, is the medium for describing the surface of things. The eye sight records outlines and contexts of places and people by means of intense contemplation, by *looking* as a form of *thinking*. That intense contemplation has two effects: it can change the look of the thing being seen because of the emotion in the contemplation, or it can trigger the imagination to reproduce other images, often hallucinatory. The surface reality does not remain either surface or real. The vision and the imagination change the look and immediate meaning of the real. Abstract concepts, such as time, are repeated, transformed, and varied, controlled at all times by Robbe-Grillet's imagination, which invents a constantly changing route and directs readers and audiences down that route. The route can be called a *motif*, and the use of motifs (to be discussed later) creates patterns within each work.

Patterns are very important in Robbe-Grillet's work since they take the place of cause and effect or of action and resolution. The patterns, although they can be traced and described, do not result in a final statement of truth:

> For us (new novelists) on the contrary, all structure would be constituted of non-meaning (anecdotal or profound meaning, it is all the same), able to do nothing but annihilate while digesting its own structural organization.... [S]tructure—for us—can only fleetingly become the place for a precarious, slipping meaning, always ready to collapse.[8]

Patterns create the structures of his works, and metonymy and motifs (or motives, as in music rather than human psychology) create the patterns. Motives do not give internal meaning to his stories nor are there "chance" elements that he does not control. His techniques are conscious, his goals are controlled, as much as the goals of experiencing novels or films can be controlled by the creator.

Structure/Pattern/Generator/Motive

Structures and patterns in Robbe-Grillet's works evolve and are not imposed. *Generators*, as he calls them, are the starting points for the evolution; they provide the inspiration, and, in all senses, the motives and controlling ideas for the movement and linkage of

1 / ORIGINS AND ATTITUDES

the parts of each work. He has used generators from literature, from art, from language, and from the external world. The myths he uses as generators come from classical literature and from popular literature; the fictional situations are stereotypical situations in literature; the artworks are real works by real artists; the places are real places. The starting points are not invented and are not free of the world and its creations. He thus acknowledges his links to society (past and present), to art, to language, and to the existing reality of the world. Nevertheless, he considers that all of these established forms are elements of an outmoded ideology, an unquestioned ideology, and that he, as an artist, must challenge outmoded ideologies. If he tentatively has a mission (a slippery mission), it is to challenge old forms, primarily by inventing new forms and by making readers/spectators aware of his inventions:

> One can only work against ideology on the one hand by pointing it out, and on the other hand, in making it grind so that it can be heard, so that it will not be innocent, so that it will lose in fact that beautiful mask of innocence and of being natural.[9]

To Robbe-Grillet, "innocence" and "naturalness" in art are negative or hypocritical states of mind. Artists and audiences must be made aware of the sources of their ideology and must also become aware that the process of making art is not effortless. Art is made by plans and with a purpose. Robbe-Grillet has, he says, "a well-thought-out distrust of everything that exalts writing as a *natural* activity."[10]

First, there may be inspiration—in his case, often through generators; but the movement onward of the generation is never self-perpetuating. The writer's will dominates the choice of material, and when chance elements interrupt the choice, they are controlled. A writer forces his invention on the material:

> To tell a tale seems to Balzac a natural and innocent work; Flaubert is without doubt one of the first writers of the 19th century to have felt violently that nothing can be natural in writing. And current sociologists have not failed to establish a parallel between this loss of confidence of the novelist in the naturalness of his word and the loss of confidence of the bourgeoisie [sic] in the legitimacy of *his* powers....

> There is not a natural order, neither moral, nor political, nor narrative; there only exist human orders created by men, with all that that assumes of the provisionary and arbitrary. (160)

Because of Robbe-Grillet's conviction that there are human orders that are provisionary and arbitrary, but nonetheless forms of order, he cannot escape the pressures of human society in his writing. When he uses pornographic or erotic subjects, he is recognizing society's obsessions and popular fantasies. When exotic places form the background of his works, he is expanding popular misconceptions or mythological inventions to create his invented settings. Picture postcards, which use real places and reduce them to flat and unrealistic surfaces, are also, according to Robbe-Grillet, effective generators for developing counterideological motifs (160).

Myths, exotic places, and popular art forms have produced for him an ironic awareness of society and a need to counter the ideological smugness and hypocrisies of society. But he also uses real places and works of art to inspire his imagination. Tunisia and Istanbul are real places where he has lived. But as settings for the novels and films, Istanbul and Tunisia become transformed into what Robbe-Grillet calls "dream images."[11] The transformation is done by isolation of details in the setting, by use of the settings as the contexts for ambiguous and mysterious actions, by verbal suggestions, and by other devices that do not change the phenomenological appearance of the places.

The photographs of David Hamilton and the paintings of René Magritte have also served Robbe-Grillet as visual inspirations or generators for his texts.[12] The paintings or photographs are described, in a fragmentary and provisional way, and then texts and artworks are juxtaposed in a single volume, in two of his later works that he does not identify as "novels." Yet flashes of stories suddenly appear from his descriptions and juxtapositions:

> The figures become alive, the repetition of a theme becomes a diachronic development, the title of a painting arises like a password.[13]

These non-novel novels, these non-art historical reflections on art, these hybrids in the interrelationship of word and image, cre-

1 / ORIGINS AND ATTITUDES

ate new environments, new self-contained universes, or, as he has proposed, new realities in the creation of art. His evolving structures (generated, inspired) have led to artistic creations that have a new identity, one more confirmation that following and controlling evolutionary patterns can produce new forms. Control is very important for him, and he has borrowed or invented various techniques to supplant the techniques that he has rejected: i.e., chronology, cause and effect, psychological or sociological logic, the integrity of an incident in time and space, expectations of intensified developments of plot and theme. Two favorite methods he has used in his novels and films are (1) the interruption of the description by contamination shots or paragraphs, and (2) the use of sonorities and rhythms in the descriptions of the events for the sake of the sound.

> In film (the contamination principle) is a system of cutting and editing which brings in increasingly long portions of "future" scenes in the midst of earlier ones.[14]

In a novel, passages of description are inserted into the work in places where they do not belong and do not seem to fit. Later, the same descriptions (or shots) are repeated in a more logical or chronological context and are expanded. In retrospect, the earlier descriptions or shots have been preparations for the expanded descriptions or shots. The major effect of the repetition is dislocation: time sequences have been shifted from their usual positions; the resulting structure is unexpected, producing shifts in reader/audience consciousness.

Contamination elements also act like memories, interpolating themselves into a narrator's consciousness because of possibly unconscious impulses. The whole effect of dislocated time, unexpected jolts of memory, and an expansion on an original image is to re-create a subjective state of mind. This subjective state of mind is not comparable to the technique of stream of consciousness. The subjective observations and descriptions are carefully, deliberately assembled, always avoiding the appearance of an objective retelling of facts and observations but never making the break between inner and outer action apparent.

Another method Robbe-Grillet has used to assemble the parts of a work (novel or film) is to make himself conscious of the sonorities (sound values) and rhythms. The deliberate assemblage of material is made on the basis of language meaning and sound. Words are carefully selected according to meaning, but then they are organized as they are presented to the reader according to sound:

> I read and re-read for several days out loud the pages that I have just written . . . to measure the deviations compared to the norm concerning the repetitions of sonorities. (420–21)

Words might be changed if certain sounds are desired, since unusual or deviant harmonies are what Robbe-Grillet is listening for. For Robbe-Grillet, the "sensuality of the text" comes from the use of language. In a film, both the sound and the image influence the pattern of assemblage. A certain quality of an early sound or a certain look of an early image will suggest a subtly harmonious (in his case, possibly unusual or deviant) sound or image for later scenes. Certain sounds or objects act like rest stops (as in music) or like coordinating punctuation marks. They link and connect the parts of the work by what Robbe-Grillet calls their "associative, connotative power" (420–21).

These processes of assemblage guarantee that the impulse to project meaning on the events and their progress in the novels and films is stifled; the reader or audience is unaware that the movement forward of the work and the effect of the movement on his/her consciousness is controlled by the author's close attention to the relationship of words, sequences of action for the sake of repetition, and the sound of the words and sequences. The author has a distinct "point of view," but it is not meant to be intellectual; his visual and aural consciousness directs his view and as much as possible his reader's/audience's view. But the author hides; within the novels and films there are specific protagonists who function as the viewers of the action. They are conscious of their environments and their own movements, and they describe them. They provide the points of view through which the audience learns about the action.

Narrator and Point of View

The narrator in each work is not telling a story but is reacting through his consciousness as he describes "what it sees, hears, or imagines."[15] Language in the form of a particular, descriptive word—usually a measuring, limiting word—is the means by which the point of view of the narrator catches the reader's attention. Point of view, for Robbe-Grillet, means the position and state of mind from which a consciousness reacts.

The narrators of the points of view are perceptive in what they see and hear, but only intermittently. As they focus on objects or people, or as they re-create scenes, they become imaginative. The perceptions become visions. Through the visions, the reader seems to be introduced into the narrator's internal universe. The reader experiences the work through the changing visions and the changing descriptions; if the reader is perceptive, he/she can also detect the ironies and incongruities. Robbe-Grillet seems to have done all he could (through his displacements and sensual development of the language) to take a nonjudgmental stance, but he does admit to an anti-ideological attitude, and there are ironic situations and characterizations in his novels and films that show that he is not a neutral observer. In an essay on *Topologie d'une cité fantôme* (*Topology of a Phantom City*), Ronald Bogue catches him out in expressing more than the "personal" formalism his statements seem to proclaim and some of his critics seem to support:

> Robbe-Grillet discounts the significance of his subject matter, I believe, not to assert a formalistic aesthetic, but to indicate that his stance toward ideology is critical rather than participatory, that he is not a sadist though his narration includes scenes of sadism.... His strategy is to remake the world after his desires, but in such a way that the world must recognize the nature and workings of its ideological structures.[16]

Susan Suleiman does not accept the idea that Robbe-Grillet uses sadism in his texts in order to teach the world about the workings of its "ideological structures." She is very skeptical that he is merely using the données of contemporary society: if he is, then "[t]he writer's activity is not only innocent, it is positively beneficial: its ultimate effect is to expose the myths for what they are, bring them up into the light, and thus deprive them of their alienating power."[17] She calls explanations that reduce sexual fantasies to cartoon images or games "rationalizations." The reader's reaction to the text, according to her analysis, has not been taken into account, and in *Project for a Revolution in New York*, the reader's reaction is encouraged to be one of sexual excitement, as men conceive of it. *Project* is a man's book in several ways: it repeats male fantasies of "omnipotence and total control over passive female bodies"; it posits a relation between language and sex ("The master is he who speaks"—my translation from Suleiman's quotation from Roland Barthes [57]); its male fantasies are oedipal. The "mother" is irrelevant or murdered and the text is self-engendered. "The role of mother has been appropriated by the one who writes; the mother's parts have become, literally, a *pre*-text. . . . [T]he ultimate masculine fantasy . . . is the fantasy of self-engenderment" (61–62).

So it seems that Robbe-Grillet's neutrality as an author is open to question; his narrators are protective devices that can be penetrated. Robbe-Grillet himself admits in *Le Miroir qui revient* (*Ghosts in the Mirror*) that "I have never spoken of anything but myself. From within, and so it has hardly been noticed. Fortunately."[18] Nevertheless, his narrators are creations that provide the tone and atmosphere of his narrations as they invoke the mystery of all creation by playing a number of roles: uncomprehending and confused, secretive and spying, deceiving and lying, metamorphic.

They play their roles through language and visualization, words and camera. Words clarify and confuse; cameras control and mesmerize. The camera looks and by certain juxtapositions suggests; the spectator participates in the camera's view of objects and spaces and their relationships to each other and to the characters also on view. Robbe-Grillet is not neutral in his expectations from readers/audience. The "spectator" needs to be aroused, to react, to participate:

> [T]he books cannot be read analytically, An active reading is required. As you (the interviewer) said, this calls the critical imagination into play. I would not only like the reader to participate in the creation of

1 / ORIGINS AND ATTITUDES 33

my story, my theme, but to participate critically as well. I don't want him to submit to the forms I elaborated on.[19]

Not submitting to his forms, as he said in this 1972 interview, may have been his goal at that time, but his films are meant to engulf the spectator so thoroughly that it becomes difficult to resist them. The experience of film watching is phenomenological and direct; the spectator is *there*:

> [The spectator can] allow himself to be carried away by the extraordinary images that he will have in front of him, by the voices of the actors, by the noises, by the music, by the rhythm of the montage, by the passion of the heroes.... [A] film addresses itself only to his sensibilities, to his faculty of seeing, of hearing, of feeling, of allowing himself to be excited.[20]

And it is true. Words and camera (camera more than words) are persuasive mediums, hard to counteract by readers/spectators, *particularly* attentive readers/spectators. The more they involve themselves in the experience of reading or filmviewing, the more difficult it is to extricate themselves and to be critical. Perhaps because of an uneasy realization of his mind/sense control (and his desire to exercise such control), Robbe-Grillet has invented the process of "slipping meaning ... a displacement of things in relation to their normal position."[21] Keeping the movement and meaning of his narratives uncertain is his technique off freeing his readers/spectators. Paradoxically, the reader/spectator cannot break free from the movement of the words and images without completely losing control over sense or sensual meaning, but he/she *must not* resolve the movement or meaning (logical or sensual) at the conclusion of the work. Paradoxically again, only a close reading of the work—noting all the techniques used and the effects of those techniques—can satisfy the need most readers/spectators have for some form of closure. The closure is intellectual but requires intense concentration of the senses on the work; nothing must be missed, and thereby hangs the sensual experience of reading (or seeing) a work by Alain Robbe-Grillet.

The next chapters are an examination of several novels and films in order to reexperience their creation and provide a sensual/critical method of participating in the act of reading (or seeing). It could be rewarding. As Wolfgang Iser said, "The need to decipher ... also entails the possibility that we may formulate ourselves and so discover what had previously seemed to elude our consciousness."[22] What may have eluded the writer's consciousness may be discovered by or in ours.

The act of reading does not demand that we psychoanalyze the author—only perhaps ourselves.

2
Confused and Misled:
The Narrator Takes Part in an Old Myth

In *The Erasers (Les Gommes)*, Robbe-Grillet's first published novel (1953), the format of the detective story provides the plot structure. The investigating detective, Wallas, is generally the experiencer of the action, but occasionally other characters' thoughts, dreams, imaginings are described. Externally, characters meet, talk, walk, and advance the action, all of which takes place in one day. But though *one day* provides the framework, the time sequences in the novel shift and slide into each other, interrupting the seemingly chronological action, juxtaposing seemingly significant pieces of "evidence" with explanations of the action. The orderly framework of *one* day conceals disorder; movement and purpose become labyrinthine.

The plot can be summarized as logical and chronological: a detective arrives in a small Flemish city (unidentified) after the supposed murder of an influential intellectual, Professor Daniel Dupont. His investigations take him to the murdered man's ex-wife, to his neighbors, and to the clinic of a doctor friend of the victim. In the meantime, the murder victim is not dead but is hiding in the clinic. The would-be assassin is confused by the death report in the newspaper, since he knows that his shot missed. The assassin and the detective frequently cover the same territory in their wanderings around the city. The detective returns to Dupont's house twenty-four hours after the supposed murder because of his suspicions, somewhat undefined and based on conflicting bits of evidence, that something is not right. Meanwhile, Dupont, the supposed victim, returns to his house to get some papers before leaving the city. Since the chief of intelligence (the detective's boss) suspects that the assassination attempt was part of a larger conspiracy, the failure of the attempt is being kept secret from everyone, including the detective, although the chief commissioner of the city begins to suspect the truth. At the house, at 7:30 P.M., the detective shoots and kills Dupont, the original supposed victim, mistaking him for the assassin.

The novel is carefully organized: a prologue, five chapters, and an epilogue, each chapter and the prologue containing numbered divisions. The prologue sets the scene of Wallas's arrival and begins the movement of time; motifs later elaborated on in the novel also appear in the prologue. Language units and sounds that recur throughout the book are used in the prologue, such as in the following description:

> Very ancient laws rule every detail of his gestures, saved for once from the uncertainty of human intentions; each second marks a pure movement: a side-step, the chair eleven inches out from the table, three wipes of the rag, half-turn to the right, two steps forward, each second marks, perfect, even, unblurred. Thirty-one. Thirty-two. Thirty-three. Thirty-four. Thirty-five. Thirty-six. Thirty-seven. Each second in its exact place.
>
> Soon unfortunately time will no longer be master. Wrapped in their aura of doubt and error, this day's events, however insignificant they may be, will in a few seconds begin their task, gradually encroaching upon the ideal order, cunningly introducing an occasional inversion, a discrepancy, a confusion, a warp, in order to accomplish their work: a day in early winter without plan, without direction, incomprehensible and monstrous.[1]

The sound rhythms of the description are created by long and short sentences, parallel phrase units, staccato phrases, and an abrupt transition between paragraphs. The rhythm is a time rhythm, precise time. Then this precise and orderly time is confused by human actions. At the beginning of the description, both the man and his actions are in harmony, and both are related to "very ancient laws" and cycles. In the second paragraph, the description shifts to the future and to the disruption of the ideal order by events. Discrepancies, inversions, and confusions, according to the description, bring about the disruptions. The order becomes disorder. The use of the future tense in the description is itself a disruption of ideal chronological time.

The ritual of cleaning is made important because of its orderliness and rhythm. Gestures and movements begin to evoke ancient rituals. By such connections, the physical act becomes a part of the natural rhythms of the day, and the description has moved from sight or perception to imagination. Another descriptive change, in the second paragraph, connects "a day in early winter" to "ideal order," since that winter's day's events will disrupt normal, if not ideal, order. The day as a day has no special value since it is nothing more than a part of a whole cycle, but events are made to seem to be in conflict with time.

The narrator of both descriptions is not clear. Words like "saved" and "unfortunately" imply a bias in favor of order, and thus the narrator is being subjective in his description. His subjectivity is further shown by the movement from realistic detail through visual perception to imaginative imagery.

Another movement from realistic detail to imaginative suggestion is in a later description that concentrates on minuteness of detail. The ordinary object, a tomato that is closely described, is no longer perceived as ordinary:

> The peripheral flesh, compact, homogeneous, and a splendid chemical red, is of an even thickness between a strip of gleaming skin and the hollow where the yellow, graduated seeds appear in a row, kept in place by a thin layer of greenish jelly along a swelling of the heart. This heart of a slightly grainy, faint pink, begins—toward the inner hollow—with a cluster of white veins, one of which extends toward the seeds—somewhat uncertainly.
>
> Above, a scarcely perceptible accident has occurred: a corner of the skin, stripped back from the flesh for a fraction of an inch, is slightly raised. (152–53)

The reader's imagination is aroused by the description because of the transformation of ordinary terms for the tomato into terms that make it seem human: skin, flesh, heart, veins, as in the phrase "skin stripped back from the flesh," which seems to describe a flayed living thing. All the nouns used—skin, flesh, heart, veins—have been used before to describe tomatoes, but in this description they are packed so closely together that each word becomes a metaphor (or a metonym), making the description seem to be a close-up view with many suggestions. An extreme close-up in a film will sometimes have a similar effect; the enlarged object becomes transformed, usually in a grotesque way.

The reader is clearly being prodded by these descriptions. The attentive reader cannot remain neutral but must be aroused sensually and imaginatively. The sound pattern of the description creates a rhythm and movement for reading the description that cannot be skimmed or summarized. The description is *not* used so that the reader can get a quick fix on the story; the story, in fact, disappears under the impact of the description since often the obvious meaning of the story is not being developed.

Exactness and orderliness in the *time* description and the accident of mutilation in the *tomato* description confuse the precision of the original flow of language. The two descriptions can be related, as the *tomato* description introduces a spatial dimension that includes stopped time: time slows down or stops in order for the elements of the object and its place in space to be absorbed. Time and space become mental experiences.

Time is a generator, and the novel evolves because of variations on the concept of time. Past-present-future and memory-fantasy-speculation are all variations on the concept that time is fourth dimensional and that it takes place in an internal as well as an external world. Thoughts and actions move back and forth between external and internal time in the novel.

Movement and Permutation in Time Relationships

Two specific clock times are important: 6:00 A.M., which marks the beginning and the end of the novel on two successive days, and 7:30 P.M., which marks the time of the murder attempt and then the time of the murder itself the next day. These times estab-

2 / CONFUSED AND MISLED   39

lish the parameters of the work; within these parameters, there are chronological events, parallel events, flashbacks, imagined events.

Prologue: Part 1 of the prologue describes the café manager's actions; then the town and its inhabitants are briefly described in part 2. A man who appeared in part 1 is described more fully in part 2. Most of part 2 is a flashback, in the present tense, to the man's actions of the evening before, from 7:00 to 7:30 P.M. Mixed in with the description of his past actions are fragments of a previous conversation that the man, Garinati, had had with his boss, Bona.

In part 3, the café manager's thoughts are triggered by a newspaper item about the murder of Daniel Dupont in his study by a burglar, which had occurred on the previous evening. He remembers that Dupont's housekeeper had used his phone (because theirs was out of order) to report the shooting, only a wound in the arm. The manager is skeptical about the newspaper report.

In part 4, Dupont is, in fact, only wounded and is in the maternity clinic of Dr. Juard with a friend, Marchat. He is aware that he is part of a terrorist plot and is hiding. He is asking Marchat to pick up some papers at his house, and Marchat resents the request.

In part 5, the commissioner of the town is introduced; he is thinking about the case; his superiors have asked him to keep out of it. Though the corpse has disappeared, the case and the previous evening's events seem to be resolved, as far as he knows.

In part 6, Garinati is also thinking about the case. But in his thoughts he knows that his actions of the previous evening have been unsuccessful, and he decides to repeat them properly. The events are clearly not resolved.

Garinati has been given the name of a special agent who has been assigned to the case; the name was in a note that he received the morning after the murder attempt, and the note seemed to assume that the attempt had been successful. Garinati is confused; or is the notewriter confused? His last thoughts are "Wallas. Special agent" (37).

Chapter 1: In part 1, Wallas is introduced. It is about 6:30 A.M., earlier than the time at which the prologue ended. The novel has backtracked. Wallas is not sure of the time because his watch stopped at 7:30 P.M. the previous evening. Wallas's memory switches to a much earlier time in his life when he had been in this town on a visit. Wallas begins to walk, and the action is described as "advancing through . . . this fragile interval" (46). By a slight emphasis on a subjective adjective to describe an abstraction ("fragile" to describe a feeling about time), the description becomes subjective. It is not clear whose subjectivity has invented the feeling of fragility, but the adjective-image is followed by an extended simile that could be describing Wallas's future state of mind.

Chapter 1, part 2 describes the mood and spirit of Wallas as he walks:

> [H]e . . . unrolls the uninterrupted ribbon of his own passage, not a series of irrational, unrelated images, but a smooth band where each element immediately takes its place in the web, even the most fortuitous, even those that might at first seem absurd or threatening or anachronistic or deceptive; they all fall into place in good order, one beside the other, and the ribbon extends without flaw or excess, in time with the regular speed of his footsteps. (48)

Wallas seems to be using the rhythm of his pace to define his control over events. His sense of time, which is translated into his movements and his measurements of his movements, gives him a feeling of freedom. Time is orderly, and order seems to satisfy his sense of freedom, especially freedom from doubt. Time and measurement are in control in his mind, and events do not seem to him to be haphazard.

Suddenly, after this description, Wallas discovers that he has been walking in a circle and has in fact wasted time and lost control of his direction. Nevertheless, when he gets some help and "re-establish[es]" his route and continues to walk, he still believes in "order and permanence" (52).

In chapter 1, part 3, details of his past—his childhood and his past work—keep coming to his mind, interrupting the continuity of his timing.

In chapter 1, part 4, as the commissioner expresses doubts about Wallas's theory, that a terrorist organization is responsible, he also

2 / CONFUSED AND MISLED

declares that he has no theory of his own and that he has not even been allowed to see the body. Listening to him, Wallas's thoughts go back to his walking and to his sense of going in a definite direction and advancing toward a goal. However, the commissioner's many suppositions about the events begin to confuse Wallas, and the direction becomes less clear.

In chapter 1, part 5, the events become even more confused by the story that another character, Dr. Juard, tells the commissioner.

In chapter 1, part 6, two events are recorded in past or past perfect tenses; they had already taken place before the present event, which is Wallas's interview with the murdered man's housekeeper. The events are also connected with disruptions in Wallas's sense of order because of his feeling of growing hunger and discomfort, his unexpected feeling of guilt in response to Dr. Juard's nurse's skeptical expression, and his present interview with the housekeeper, which induces a flashback to the visit to Dr. Juard's clinic. His watch is still stopped at 7:30, and the bronze clock in Dupont's bedroom is also stopped.

Chapter 2: In part 1, another character, who has already been mentioned, appears in person: Bona, Garinati's boss. During his conversation with Garinati, Bona gives a different version of the events from what Garinati thinks he knows. Garinati is still confused about whether to believe what he saw.

In chapter 2, part 2, Garinati closes the door and the latch falls. He begins to search for Wallas.

In chapter 2, part 3, Wallas closes the door of Dupont's house and the latch falls. The acts are paralleled, though the time relationship is not clear. Another shift in time occurs when Wallas fantasizes that his chief is now in charge of the investigation instead of himself. His imagination is now making his insecurity evident. Another exercise in imagination is described when Wallas is questioning a witness. She visualizes an event in her mind (after he has asked some suggestive questions) and then she relates that visualized event to Wallas. Both Wallas and the reader are momentarily skeptical about the reality of the occurrence.

In chapter 2, part 4, confusion about events and time is rampant. At the café, a drunken habitué insists that he has seen Wallas before but can't remember the time or the place. The commissioner's earlier joke that Wallas is a suspect is remembered, presumably by Wallas. In the drunk's imagination, he remembers pursuing Wallas. In the café, he grabs Wallas and falls down. When he is questioned, he is confused about the previous night's events. When the manager acts suspicious about Wallas, Wallas would like to show his police identity card but decides not to because he looks older in the photo on the card. A future tense is used to describe the actions of the next few minutes: water dripping from the faucet with "metronymic regularity" *will be* turned off by the proprietor, and the "scene *will be* over" soon (120), as though all the action described had been a performance.

In chapter 2, part 5, paragraphs of description are juxtaposed in an unexplained order: the manager's fantasies as he stares into space; Bona's patience as he waits for another conspirator; Garinati's visit to the café and his questioning of the manager; Wallas's departure from the café. The time relationships are not clear, though the paragraphs follow each other without interruption or transitional words.

In chapter 2, part 6, Wallas starts to walk in the wrong direction but soon reverses himself. At the end of the chapter, approximately in the middle of the book, there is a description in which times and places are combined in both a real and an imaginary context. The description involves a display in a shop window. It consists of a painting, a mannequin of a painter, and a photograph of a contemporary city from which the mannequin seems to be making a drawing. However, the drawing she is making is an ancient landscape. Everything is linked by ambiguities: the mannequin looks like a real artist and the action seems to be one of copying, but the links are all false. The mannequin is not real, and it is not copying a photograph.

Chapter 3: In part 1, a scene is described in the present tense. It is an imaginative reenactment of the central murder event, imagined by the commissioner of the town. He is groping for a solution. No matter how he organizes the events in his mind, the results are unsatisfactory. Having refused to accept either the official or the secret version of the event, he is resorting to hypothesis; his

2 / CONFUSED AND MISLED 43

hypotheses are ridiculous and do not at all accurately summon up the real event. However, the official version is also false, although deliberately.

Another imaginative excursion into the future occurs when Dupont's friend, the merchant Marchat, envisions the consequences of the promise he had made to Dupont the previous evening. His fears are real to him, but his vision of the consequences of his promise seems as ridiculous as the commissioner's hypotheses.

In chapter 3, part 2, Marchat's fears and visions of the future become worse.

In chapter 3, part 3, Wallas is again feeling unwell, and his senses seem inordinately sensitive. He lapses into fantasies and memories, like almost everyone else in this chapter. In the post office, he is mistaken for someone else, thus increasing his confusion and distress.

In chapter 3, part 4, the commissioner, in talking to Wallas, continues to dismiss all the other evidence in favor of his own hypotheses.

In chapter 3, part 5, Wallas tries to enter imaginatively into the commissioner's hypotheses by visualizing the murder in a different way from the official version. But he doubts his own vision. He continues his walk around the city, gets lost, and in a small bookstore in which he goes to ask directions, he also asks for a soft eraser. Two descriptions then recall two of his memories: the window display and his conversation with the saleswoman in the Victor Hugo bookstore. However, the description of the window display has been transformed (in his memory?), and the conversation inspires a thought: the saleswoman is the ex-Mme. Dupont.

Chapter 4: In part 1, an unidentified man at an unidentified time is watching a cable floating in the waters of the canal.

In chapter 4, part 2, Wallas speculates about the events of the past, after a second conversation with the Victor Hugo bookstore saleswoman. Wallas almost meets Garinati, who has entered the shop during Wallas's conversation and has bought a postcard reproduction of the photo of Dupont's house.

In chapter 4, part 3, the post office employees are questioned, and the resemblance between Wallas and someone they call André WS (VS in the French), who has a box at the post office, is stressed. Another hypothesis about the "murdered" man's past is made when another investigator's report is read by the commissioner, and the report is re-created as an imaginary scene. It is not clear whose imagination is re-creating the scene.

In chapter 4, part 4, the commissioner rejects his assistant's report and wants "the truth . . . the truth . . . the truth" (198).

In chapter 4, part 5, Madame Jean, a post office employee, insists in her thoughts that Wallas is André WS.

In chapter 4, part 6, a description of a train station where a worried Dr. Juard is waiting to meet Wallas becomes a climactic evocation of the rhythms and movements of time that have served as major structural elements in the book:

> A tremendous voice fills the hall. Projected by invisible loudspeakers, it bounces back and forth against the walls covered with signs and advertisements, which amplify it still more, multiply it, reflect it, baffle it with a whole series of more or less conflicting echoes and resonances, in which the original message is lost—transformed into a gigantic oracle, magnificent, indecipherable, and terrifying.
>
> As suddenly as it had begun, the uproar stops, again making way for the confused murmur of the crowd.
>
> People are hurrying in all directions. They must have guessed—or imagined they guessed—the meaning of the announcement, for the agitation has redoubled. Among the curtailed movements—each of which affects only a small section of the hall—between a time-table and a ticket window, from an information booth to a newsstand—or even within less defined areas, animated here and there with less vague, hesitant, discontinuous, aleatory movements—in the middle of this swarming mass occasionally interrupted, up to now, by some less episodic trajectory, distinct currents now appear; in one corner a single file has started across the entire hall in a decisive diagonal; farther on scattered impulses unite in a series of calls and quick steps whose impetus clears a wide passage until it comes to a halt against one of the exits. (200)

2 / CONFUSED AND MISLED   45

In this description, not specifically assigned to any particular narrator, the phrases are either divided into small units or organized so that they proceed with a forward rush. The style imitates the structuring of movement with which the description is concerned. Sounds also move. They are described as "amplifi[ed]," "reflect[ed]," and baffle[d]." They culminate in an image of an oracle—"magnificent, indecipherable, and terrifying." In a clear parody of classical tragedy, this oracle delivers an incomprehensible message to its listeners, which they presumably interpret as suits them. Like the events in the novel, the sound and movement are at first orderly but then become aleatory. The description involves the reader in the experience of the movement, by the phrasing and visual imagery: "a single file," "scattered impulses," "quick steps."

Dr. Juard's waiting is generally described in time and rhythm units. He takes a certain number of steps in one direction. He stops for a few seconds. His thoughts trace the events from the past to his present situation. He resolves his fears momentarily with the comment, "Yet nothing has happened yet today. Time is passing quite normally" (203).

Time begins to close in on him more violently during the last part of his waiting. A sign urges people to "tak(e) *The Times*"; Wallas, for whom he is waiting, is late, and Dr. Juard's fears begin again; Juard then decides he hasn't "a moment to lose" (204).

In chapter 4, part 7, Garinati is also waiting, and he arranges and rearranges objects on a mantel. Later, as he walks, his mind mingles memories, imagined events, and his present actions. This description is a repetition of an earlier description—in chapter 4, part 1—in which Garinati was not identified.

Chapter 5; In part 1, the time is night, and Wallas is again walking. Then a sequence of actions that occurred prior to this action is described. Several of Wallas's memories are described. His meeting with Juard, previously described, is briefly retold. The part ends in a description of the action immediately preceding his present walk: Wallas leaves the café pursued by the drunk, who is asking him a riddle.

In chapter 5, part 2, Wallas is speaking to the commissioner, who shows him a communication on a postcard, on which is a reproduction of the photo in the stationery-bookstore window. As Wallas leaves the commissioner, he remembers the figure of the man who bought such a postcard as Wallas was visiting Dupont's ex-wife. He thinks of the ex-wife (Evelyne), of the conversation in the store, and of Dupont's house. All of these memories concern actions already described in chapter 5, part 1, and all of the actions occurred either during or preceding his walk, which took place that evening.

In chapter 5, part 3, as Wallas still walks toward Dupont's house, he remembers a scene in a "Pompeian-style city" (203) that he realizes was the city he visited with his mother in his childhood, and he remembers that the city he is now visiting is that very place. His mother's image becomes confused with that of the saleswoman Evelyne. Wallas arrives at Dupont's house at 7:00 P.M. He repeats actions that were previously described as having been performed by Garinati in chapter 1, part 2, when Garinati tried to assassinate Dupont, but Wallas changes the actions slightly. He does what Garinati forgot to do: he turns off the light in the study as he waits for the person he thinks is the murderer.

In chapter 5, part 4, tension is introduced as the scene shifts to the commissioner, who now has an idea and tries to call Wallas.

In chapter 5, part 5, the tension increases as Dupont leaves the clinic where he has been hiding and then stops at his house to pick up some papers before he leaves the city. The time covered is brief and the actions are described in detail. The last action is the firing of the revolver at Dupont by Wallas.

In chapter 5, part 6, Wallas's watch has started at 7:30 P.M., precisely twenty-four hours after it had stopped. He calls the commissioner on Dupont's telephone, which has been out of order for four days but is now suddenly working, and he receives the last clue to the mystery. But it is too late.

Epilogue: It is 6:00 A.M. Again, the manager is arranging the café. Wallas has just come in and has gone to his room. Garinati comes in and asks for Wallas but leaves without seeing him. Garinati has already seen Dupont's corpse. Wallas is planning to leave the city and has already decided to resign his investigative job. Garinati plans to follow Wallas.

In the final scenes, fragments of conversation and fragments of description are joined, like bits of time and events trying to fit into the puzzle of the day's happenings.

Tightening the Construction; Freeing the Imagination

A number of methods have been used to link the nonlinear flow of time described in the preceding analysis: parallel actions; blending of past and present from paragraph to paragraph in each part; juxtaposition of present action, memory, imaginative re-creation, fantasy, and explanation; shift of consciousness from a present moment to a fantasized moment and then back again; repetition of scenes, sometimes with a slight variation.

Order, in this aleatory though connected flow of time, is parodied, and the main character, Wallas, who has a great anxiety about order and the narrowest confines of logic, is the principal victim of the parody. When Wallas is unable to follow the clues in an orderly way, he is confused and his thoughts become uncontrolled. His circular movement when he walks around the city, often losing his way, shows the form of his confusion, its purposeless and unimaginative direction.

Robbe-Grillet likes ambiguities. In a tightly constructed and very controlled work of art, he plays games with order. He also plays games with the use of symbols and other forms of imaginative imagery. At the beginning, middle, and end of the novel, there are descriptions involving mirrors and water. From the beginning:

> A fat man is standing here, the manager, trying to get his bearings among the tables and chairs. Over the bar, the long mirror where a sick image floats, the manager, greenish, his features blurred, liverish and fleshy in his aquarium.

> On the other side, behind the mirror, the manager again who dissolves slowly in the dawning light from the street. It is no doubt this silhouette that has just put the café in order, now it need only disappear. In the mirror flickers the reflection of this ghost, already almost completely decomposed; and beyond, increasingly undecided, the waver-

ing rigmarole of shadows: the manager, the manager, the manager. . . . The manager, a mournful nebula, drowned in his halo. (8)

Later, the manager watches himself in the mirror and grimaces; his face "freezes in a gargoyle mask" (11). In both descriptions, the mirror is the intermediary in the transformation of the image of the manager. The image changes from direct representation of the manager to reflection in a mirror, and then to an illusionistic, ghost-like existence on the other side of the mirror or to transformation in the mirror.

In the middle of the book, water, which also reflects and distorts, is the means for capturing, distorting, and changing an image:

> In the murky water of the aquarium, furtive shadows pass—an undulation whose vague existence dissolves of its own accord . . . and afterward it is questionable whether there had been anything to begin with. But the dark patch reappears and makes two or three circles in broad daylight, soon coming back to melt, behind a curtain of algae, deep in the protoplasmic depths. A last eddy, dying quickly away, makes the mass tremble for a second. Again everything is calm . . . until suddenly a new form emerges and presses its dream face against the glass . . . Pauline, sweet Pauline . . . and no sooner does it appear than it vanishes in its turn, to make way for other spectors and phantoms. (120)

The ghost or dream image that is evoked by the swirling waters of the aquarium is another person (Pauline), who is a product, probably, of the manager's memories; but the immediate memory disappears and has no meaning for the events in the novel. At the end of the book the aquarium evokes images that express vague, undefined feelings, just as the previous images and memories were not well defined, but this final uncertain imagery captures the evanescent nature of the reality created by the book.

> In the troubled water of the aquarium, furtive shadows pass. The manager is motionless at his post. His massive body leans on his outspread arms; his hands grip the edge of the bar; his head hangs down, almost threatening, the mouth somewhat twisted, the gaze blank. Around him the familiar specters dance their waltz, like moths circling

a lampshade and bumping into it, like dust in the sun, like little boats lost at sea, lulling to the sea's rhythm in their delicate cargo, the old casks, the dead fish, the rigging and tackle, the buoys, the stale bread, the knives and the men. (256)

The coarse manager and the delicate specters are juxtaposed in rhythmical phrases, in a musical flourish of imaginative evocations. These final images are not connected to the main theme of the novel but to the seacoast atmosphere of the Flemish town and the insubstantiality of the events of the story.

The beginning, middle, and end descriptions of the aquarium and mirror are links holding together the form and variations of the novel; they turn our attention to the novel's coherence as a work of art, not as a story with beginning, climax, and resolution. In this early novel, the plot does have a resolution, that is, the prefigured killing of Daniel Dupont. But who are the terrorists and what happens to them? Why does Garinati follow Wallas? Many elements are unexplained, open-ended.

There are other links creating a coherence in the work, especially those elements parodying the connections to the myth of Oedipus. Wallas, the "Oedipal" figure, remembers having been in this city earlier in his life; his memories occur and reoccur on pages 42, 55, 130, and 230. Each recurrence expands the original memory. There are repetitions and variations on a riddle, asked by the drunk in the café on pages 13, 114, 226, and 255. The first riddle is the same one asked of Oedipus: "What is the animal that, in the morning" (13). But the second riddle is completely unrelated to the first one: "What is the difference between a train . . . a train and a bottle of wine?" (114). The suggested parallel to the ancient myth turns into a joke in the second riddle, but a third riddle becomes a comment on the action (and on the confusions in the development of the action): "What is the animal that is a parricide in the morning, incestuous in the afternoon, and blind in the evening? . . . No . . . blind in the morning, incestuous in the afternoon, a parricide in the evening" (226). The fourth riddle returns to an animal image that is completely irrelevant to the myth: "What animal is black, has six legs, and flies?" (255). The riddle shifts from suggestive symbol to innocuous joke at the moment that Wallas gets the idea that it might have some significance for his actions: he has killed Daniel Dupont, though it is almost certain that Dupont is not the father that he and his mother were searching for in this city many years ago. Wallas's connection to Evelyne, Dupont's ex-wife, who could have been Wallas's stepmother, is also false. But false or not, the possibilities and the parallelism make the killing of Dupont by Wallas a mockery of the myth.

Other "clues" about the suggestions that this story is connected to the myth of Oedipus constantly recur: the design on the embroidered curtain of a child and some shepherds, the representation in the drawing in the store window of the ruins of Thebes, the vague memory that the name of the eraser has *di* in the middle. Like the drawbridges that cross the canals in the city and link the streets to each other in the city's circular layout, the clues lead the reader in circles. The connection to Oedipus is ironic rather than thematic.

Another bit of ironic humor is in the title—*Les Gommes*, in French. Gommes could be gum-shoe detectives (suggested by Morrissette), gum erasers, or even gummed-up works, such as the confusions and blockages in the heads of the investigators.[2] Gum erasers wipe out words and meanings, just as the final action wipes out the meaning of the terrorist plot.

There are other indications that the symbols that should lead to a significant parallelism to the Oedipus myth really reflect other kinds of blindness. Descriptions of eyeglasses, either dark tinted or light tinted or with one lens of each, are on pages 186, 239, and 244. If the Oedipus parallelism were significant for the meaning of the story, these descriptions are references to blindness or semiblindness; but as appears in the gummed-up action, they more accurately refer to the semivision and semiunderstanding that characterize the investigation. If there is any subterranean theme in the novel, it is the theme of incompetence and stupidity. Wallas's confusions underscore this idea: on page 197, the commissioner's assistant says, "Sometimes you go through hell and high water to find a murderer ... when all you need to do is stretch out your hand." Wallas remembers the statement in this way: "Sometimes you go through hell and high water to find a murderer, and the crime hasn't even been committed. You go through hell and high water to discover it . . . quite far from him, whereas one need only point to one's own chest" (253).

The music of the text controls the use and repetition of imagistic elements more than their meaning for the story: descriptions of the flotsam on the canal (superficially resembling a sphinx form) occur on pages 22 and 32; descriptions of Dupont's house and the area around it are on pages 16, 20, 35, 36, and 235. An examination of a passage of description as written in the original French will show some of the sound and language patterns Robbe-Grillet uses intermittently, along with his fantasized images:

> (1) . . . Le mouvement d'un bras, la musique de mots perdus, Pauline, la douce Pauline. (2) La douce Pauline, morte d'étrange façon, il y a bien longtemps. (3) Etrange? (4) Le patron se pench vers la glace. (5) Que voyez-vous donc la d'étrange? . . . (10) Les yeux de Pauline. (11) Etrange?[3]

Repetition—*Pauline, étrange* (strange, odd)—triggers a train of thought and then comes back to the original sounds and suggestions: *les yeux de Pauline* (the eyes of Pauline), and *étrange* (strange). The descriptions are broken into phrase units in the sentences and become musical rather than rational. The letter *m* recurs often in the first two sentences and is repeated in words used in the omitted sentences: *malveillante* (malevolent), *mort* (death), *masque* (mask), *monstre* (monster). The sound of words and phrases is a far more important linking device in the novel than the development of a theme. Themes may or may not be detected, as it suits the reader, but the flow of language and the cohesion of the parts of the work must be recognized and felt in order to experience the work, and many forms of linkage are used to bring about that experience.

Making Connections by Ironic Doubling

No character or event escapes involvement in the ambiguous movement of the novel, primarily by the use of doubling and pairing. Four sets of names of characters are paired, resulting in misunderstandings and confusions about the events. The pairings are Daniel Dupont/Albert Dupont; Evelyne Dupont/Wallas's Mother; Wallas/Garinati; and Wallas/André WS (VS).

The first misunderstanding resulting from a pairing occurs when someone tells the manager that Albert Dupont has been killed, although the manager knows that it is Daniel Dupont who has been killed. At the end of the novel, Albert Dupont is indeed killed, as is Daniel again, but there is a discrepancy in the two deaths: Albert has been hit by a car, and Daniel has been shot. Thus, the original bearer of the news has inaccurately predicted the means but accurately predicted the results. The two deaths prompt a joke from one of the habitués of the café: "You're not trying to tell us," Antoine says, "that someone named Dupont gets killed every night" (254). The joke is not a prediction about future events; the book is finished with the second death.

The second misunderstanding occurs with Evelyne, the saleswoman in the Victor Hugo stationery shop (in the window of which is displayed the mannequin who is dressed like a painter painting the ruins of Thebes and using a photo of Daniel Dupont's house, as though she is copying it). Wallas has two conversations with Evelyne, the second after he has realized that she is Daniel Dupont's ex-wife. She is young, perhaps five or at the most ten years older than Wallas, and she behaves seductively to him.

As he remembers the visit that he made to this city with his mother when he was a child, Evelyne's image gets confused with that of his mother. He also remembers that he was coming to see his father, whom he really did not know. His past and present experiences blend the images of his mother and Evelyne, as perhaps his feeling for his mother blends into his attraction for Evelyne, with her "little throaty laugh" (231). Wallas did not really know his father, just as Dupont is said to have fathered a son whom he does not know, or want to acknowledge. The identification of Wallas's situation with that of the hypothetical son (who is given the name Jean in an imaginative speculation by Wallas) is ironically completed when Wallas performs the act that he had imagined Jean had performed—the killing of Dupont.

Neither Wallas's mother nor Jean ever appears in reality in the book, nor is there a confusion of identities between Mother/Evelyne and Wallas/Jean based on physical resemblance or emotional empathy. On the other hand, the pairings of Wallas with Garinati and with André WS do involve mistaken identity and parallelism of action and situation.

Garinati is Wallas's double because they perform parallel actions. Wallas completes the deed that Garinati bungled, in turn bungling his investigation. In some descriptions, their actions connect them very closely. In the prologue, part 2, there is a description of Dupont's house and grounds when Garinati is arriving to assassinate Dupont: "the iron fence, the spindle tree hedge, the gravel path around the house" (16). Later, in chapter 1, part 6, when Wallas goes to the house to see the housekeeper after the supposed assassination, a description traces his route as he approaches and enters the house, and the same objects are described: "Wallas follows the hedge, behind the iron fence, and stops at the gate. . . . He closes the gate, follows the gravel path" (81). The routes they take through the house itself are similar. Another blending of action is suggested by the closing of a door and the fall of a latch:

> The latch clicks as it falls back into place. . . . Garinati hesitates in front of the door he has just shut behind him. (100–101)
>
> Wallas, already half turned around, hears the latch fall back into place; he lets go of the doorknob and looks up at the house opposite. (102)
>
> Fabius, having closed the garden gate behind him, inspects the premises. . . . [H]e immediately looks away. . . . [W]ithout wasting time he crosses the canal. (103)

The three descriptions connect the assassin, the inspector who is the potential assassin, and the inspector's boss (who would not make Wallas's mistakes). The first two descriptions are of real actions, performed about twelve hours apart, but the third description is a fantasy in Wallas's mind as he speculates on the inadequacy of his own investigation. Wallas, as the descriptions indicate and as some of his actions illustrate, resembles the assassin, and both would like to resemble their chiefs. Wallas's metamorphosis into an assassin completes the resemblance and the action of the novel. If he had been more like his chief, the story would have concluded differently.

Another assassin who is part of the terrorist band led by Bona is the shadowy André WS (or VS) whom we never meet. He resembles Wallas in height, build, and clothing. The drunk, the woman in the apartment across from Dupont's house, and the girl in the post office all think that Wallas is the stranger whom they have seen near Dupont's house and in the post office picking up suspicious-looking mail. The mail that Wallas is mistakenly given at the post office is addressed to André WS. WS (or even VS) sounds like Wallas. This identification increases the suspicions that seem to dog Wallas's actions all through the novel. His own insecurities are heightened by these suspicions. They disturb his identity as well as his sense of order and direction.

Plot and point of view are almost identical in this novel, the primary point of view being Wallas's, and the dominating plot line being his confused experiences and conceptions. Other points of view occasionally contribute to the confusion of action, mainly through the imaginings of the manager, Garinati, and Bona, but they do not serve to make these characters more real for the readers or their thoughts more revelatory for the line of action. They furnish the novel with decorations of description, with experiments in word arrangement, with information that is contradictory and confusing, and the contradictions create the tensions in the movement of the novel—real tensions toward unresolved resolutions. Perhaps they also point to the magic of language, as is indicated in one of Garinati's possible musings: "It is merely a matter of following the text, reciting phrase after phrase, and the words will be fulfilled and Lazarus will rise from his tomb, wrapped in his shroud" (19).

Another image in his musings seems to be predicting Robbe-Grillet's future involvement with film as theatre:

> In this setting determined by law, without an inch of land to the right or left, without a second's hesitation, without resting, without looking back, the actor suddenly stops, in the middle of a phrase.... He knows it by heart, this role he plays every evening; but today he refuses to go any farther. Around him the other characters freeze, arm raised or leg half bent. The measure begun by the musicians goes on and on. (19)

2 / CONFUSED AND MISLED

The actor's refusal to continue his role is related to the "fragile interval" and to the extended simile that explains it and that is experienced by Wallas as he walks around the city:

> The only pedestrian, Wallas advances through this fragile interval. (Just as a man who has stayed up too late often no longer knows to which date to ascribe this dubious time, when his existence loses its shape; his brain, tired out by work and waking, tries in vain to reconstitute the series of days: he is supposed to have finished for the next day this job begun last night, between yesterday and tomorrow there is no place left for the present. Completely exhausted, he finally throws himself down on his bed and falls asleep. Later, when he wakes up, he'll find himself in his normal today. (46–47)

Later, when Wallas recovers his sense of himself, his feelings are those of the actor continuing his role: "For it is Wallas who is advancing; it is to his own body that this movement belongs, not to the backcloth some stagehand might be unrolling" (48).

Art time and art reality are the provinces of the artist, as distinct from real time and real existence; art is what the artist does, incorporating and transforming his material. A central image, perhaps a significant statement of Robbe-Grillet's aesthetic philosophy, is the window display in the stationery bookstore. It is fully described in the middle of the book:

> [I]t represents an "artist" drawing "from nature."... [S]tepping back slightly to see both his work and the model at the same time, he is putting the finishing touches on a carefully drawn landscape—which must actually be a copy of some master. It is a hill with the ruins of a Greek temple among cypress trees; in the foreground, fragments of columns lie scattered here and there; in the distance, in the valley, appears a whole city with its triumphal arches and palaces—rendered, despite the distance and the accumulation of buildings, with a scrupulous concern for detail. ... But in front of the man, instead of the Hellenic countryside, stands ... an immense photographic print of a crossroads in a twentieth-century city. (125)

In this display, art and reality are not related to each other, as is stated in a series of oppositions: drawing of an ancient landscape/photograph of a contemporary scene; drawing "from nature"/copying an image from memory or imagination; a hill with scattered ruins/a city with arches and many buildings. Later in the novel, the same window display is described, but the description has crucial differences from its predecessor:

The ruins of Thebes.

On a hill above the city, a Sunday painter has set up his easel in the shade of cypress trees, between the scattered shafts of columns. He paints carefully, his eyes shifting back to his subject every few seconds; with a fine brush he points up many details that are scarcely noticeable to the naked eye, but which assume a surprising intensity once they are reproduced in the picture. He must have very sharp eyes. One could count the stones that form the edge of the quay, the bricks of the gable-end, and even the slates in the roof. At the corner of the fence, the leaves of the spindle trees gleam in the sun, which emphasizes their outlines. Behind, a bush rises above the hedge, a bare bush whose every twig is lined with a bright streak where the light hits it, and a dark one on the shadow side. The snapshot has been taken in winter, on an exceptionally clear day. (168–69)

The Hellenic landscape is now clearly identified as Thebes (the Oedipal connection). The painter is part of the landscape and is painting rather than drawing the scene supposedly before him. But the scene before him is not his model; he is painting a scene from a modern city, in which there is a quay, a street, and a house. As the description continues, the scene he is painting is Dupont's house and street corner (as previously described in other parts of the novel), and in fact the last sentence returns to the photograph of the house, also mentioned earlier. The painter's painting and the snapshot are blended. Several levels of blending occur in this smooth-flowing description: the ancient past, the realistic present given in scrupulous detail, the supposed re-creation of a scene in a painting, the actual re-creation of a scene from a photograph. The art described here is visual art, but it is in the context of the verbal art of the novel and is blended into that context, encouraged by the blending and flow of sentences. The author, Robbe-Grillet, is encouraging and leading the reader,. who cannot for the moment escape from the flow of words. By being bound to the flow of words, the reader experiences the work and the "meaning," as Wolfgang Iser says:

> [I]t is in the reader that the text comes to life, and this is true even when the "meaning" has become so historical that it is no longer relevant to us. In reading we are able to experience things that no longer exist and to understand things that are totally unfamiliar to us.[4]

Though Robbe-Grillet does not make many distinctions of character or sensitivity among his characters—in fact encouraging us to see them as indistinguishable by his doublings—occasionally he will give insights and aesthetic experiences to a character whom the reader does not really know, such as to the manager and, in one description, to Bona, the chief assassin:

> Usually this landscape has little relief and looks rather unattractive, but this morning the grayish yellow sky of snowy days gives it unaccustomed dimensions. Certain outlines are emphasized, others are blurred; here and there distances open out, unsuspected masses appear; the whole view is organized into a series of planes silhouetted against one another, so that the depth, suddenly illuminated, seems to lose its natural look—and perhaps its reality—as if this overexactitude were possible only in painting. Distances are so affected that they become virtually unrecognizable, without its being possible to say in just what way they are transformed: extended or telescoped—or both at once—unless they have acquired a new quality that has more to do with geometry. (95)

It is easier to explain perceptual transformation in a description of a visual scene than in a description of an event or a concept; in a narrative, the rendering (author) and the receiving (reader) consciousnesses present and experience constant transformations in the context of a verbal work of art. The transformations are like transformations in visual perception: blurring of images, intrusions of "unexpected masses," a change in the depth and reality of an event (especially as previously noted because of "overexactitude"), confusion of distances or distancing (our relationship to the characters and events).

The reader seems to be given clues to the reading of this form of art—and to later works by this artist. The many surface descriptions change the depth and reality of the natural object, and generators and motifs—the detective story, the Oedipus story, the transformations in the concept of time, the confusions of characters with each other—complicate the descriptions beyond conventional meaning.

The Erasers, Robbe-Grillet's first published novel, is closest to the traditional novel in its outward form. Something does happen; something is completed. The generators and motifs keep the action moving as the actions seem to change. Even the hero is related to the image of an antihero, at least the antihero of antiquity and commedia del'arte—the fool, the blunderer.

The comedy and humor in Robbe-Grillet's work has received some attention, particularly by him in interviews.[5] It takes the form of parody, mockery, and some puns and tongue-in-cheek comments; he suggests that he is connecting his sense of play and irony to questions about himself, to questions about conflicts within himself:

> If I am pursuing an enigma that appears to me as a lack in my own meaningful continuity, how could I possibly give a full, unbroken account of it? How could I express such a paradoxical relation to the world and to my own being "simply," a relation in which everything is ambiguous, contradictory, fleeting?[6]

His humor is paradoxical, contradictory, anticlimactic. He plays games with word meanings ("gumshoes," "gummed-up works"), and the fantasies of his characters produce false possibilities about the puzzle of the events.[7] *The Erasers* is a parody and a mockery of the contemporary desire to see the truths of behavior and plot as timeless. The ideology of timelessness is questioned in life and literature. The iconoclasm of *The Erasers* is decipherable, if ambiguous, on the narrative level; in later works, Robbe-Grillet challenges the narrative form by using more obtrusive narrators, by further limiting the action of the narrative, and by confusing the coherence of any sort of fictional reality through the use of previously written works, especially those based on other people's artworks.

3
The Hidden *I* and the Camera Eye: Novels and a Film Re-create Obsession

Jealousy (*La Jalousie*, 1957), *In the Labyrinth* (*Dans le labyrinthe*, 1959), novels, and the film *The Immortal One* (*L'Immortelle*, 1963) are almost entirely described or seen as projections of internal states of mind. In all these works, the psychology is one of obsession, established by Robbe-Grillet's techniques of repetition, flashes of scenes forward and backward, compulsive counting and measuring, confusions, contradictions. Space—the distribution of objects within boundaries and places—and time—the movement of events as perceived by a consciousness—affect each other. As Roland Barthes says,

> [A]n object, described for the first time at a certain moment in the novel's progress, reappears later on, but with a barely perceptible difference. It is a difference of a situational or spatial order—what was on the right, for example, is now on the left. Time dislocates space, arranging the object like a series of slices that almost completely cover one another: and it is this spatial "almost" which contains the temporal dimension of Robbe-Grillet's object.[1]

Because of the strong interrelationships of space and time in the two novels, they unroll like film strips. The film, made later than the novels and filmed almost at the same time that *Last Year at Marienbad* was being filmed, confirms the fact that Robbe-Grillet thinks visually and turned, for a period of his life, to making movies. *L'Immortelle* was his first film as a writer and director, since his work on *Last Year at Marienbad* was limited to writing the scenario, although both Robbe-Grillet and Alain Resnais, the director, insist that they were in total agreement as to the intention and effects of the finished film.[2] *L'Immortelle* is indisputably his work in intention and effect.

The action can be summarized: a French professor, called N in the published film-novel,[3] arrives in Istanbul for a year or two of teaching. While exploring the city, he meets a beautiful young woman called Lâle, or L. She drives him around in her white convertible, and they go for a ferryboat ride on the Bosphorus, from which she points out places that have a real or imagined exotic history. They begin a love affair. She tells him almost nothing about herself, or she tells him facts that contradict her actions. He sometimes suspects that they are being watched. After she receives a message delivered by a small boy (who speaks Greek to her), she fails to keep an appointment. He begins to search for her, and in several interviews, he hears many contradictory facts and ideas from a young woman whom they both know and from several men to whom this young woman has referred him.

Unexpectedly, he sees her, Lâle, standing on the street in a bazaar area of the town. Near her is a fat man accompanied by two large grey dogs. He has seen the man and the dogs several times before. N and L drive down a secluded road in her car, and she speaks somewhat incoherently about being free. One of the large grey dogs suddenly appears in the headlights. She swerves the car and crashes into a tree. When the police arrive, she is dead, but the professor is only slightly injured; his hand is bleeding.

He wanders around their old haunts, remembering her, fantasizing about her, suspecting the past but still asking questions about her. He is rebuffed, or he hears accusations that he was responsible for her death. He sees her car for sale and he buys it. He rides down the same secluded road, sees the other large dog in the headlights, and crashes into a tree and dies. The last shot of the film is of Lâle on the deck of a ferryboat, and she is laughing.

In the ciné-roman (published film script), Robbe-Grillet seems to explain the work in "Preliminary Notes."

3 / THE HIDDEN *I* AND THE CAMERA EYE 61

> Yet Istanbul is a real city, and the young woman he meets there and the men and women he passes in the streets of the city are real men and women. But from the moment they enter into someone's head they become strictly speaking imaginary.... The same thing happens to the city. Contaminated in the popular imagination by a mixture of Pierre Loti, the Blue Guide [sic] and The Thousand and One Nights [sic], it shifts constantly from picture postcard to the obvious symbolism of chains and iron bars, remaining at the same time full of the very real bustle of ships, harbours, and crowds.[4]

Photographic images always seem real, and it is not necessary for Robbe-Grillet to explain that when the audience sees the city, the ships, the harbour, the crowds, it believes them. They are real; this is the way it looks; this can be believed. He does not have to establish their realness by detailed descriptions, but he must challenge our beliefs and our senses by re-creating the images in our heads; he must make them imaginary. *Popular* imagination is a contaminant in his creation that must be taken into account, gladly, by Robbe-Grillet. Popular images, taken from fairy tales and works of exotic fiction, are part of the tourist baggage and the expectation of excitement that tourists have. Their visual perceptions are already conditioned by myths. For Robbe-Grillet, both real and popular myths are generators for creating his work, his imagined reality.[5] The film medium is also a generator, a chance for him to challenge an audience's assumptions that only real-life stories and characters will be placed in the real settings. Film is always an illusion, but it is hard for viewers to see into the illusion, to recognize the stereotyping, the inauthenticity, of the popular images and the film medium unless it is very rudely jolted. Special effects can jolt belief (though special effects sometimes help create belief), but a stronger device of disillusionment is denial of expectation. Just as the preliminary descriptions of places in *Jealousy* and *In the Labyrinth* help draw readers into the fictional settings (before these settings are confused and mixed up with the flashforward and flashbackward use of time and the tricks of memory of the narrators), so the film images of real places help draw viewers into Robbe-Grillet's generative net:[6]

Shot 1, page 15:	The coast of the Bosphorus moves slowly past in the background: wooden houses, trees, the large towers of an old citadel.
Shot 7, page 15:	The setting is a Muslim cemetery attached to a mosque: the graves are very close together, and the funerary monuments are in a good state of repair.
Shot 8, page 16:	The setting is now an immense, deserted beach overlooked by high dunes of white sand with a few large clumps of grasslike vegetation here and there.
Shot 16, page 20:	The setting around him is a street corner, with the same wooden houses and a very small abandoned cemetery with gravestones leaning in all directions.
Shot 25, page 26:	The Bosphorus coast road, some distance away. The embankment is now lined with trees, and some large Turkish boats are anchored near the shore.
Shot 39, pages 36–37:	We are in a sort of open-air café that projects out over the water, in a city centre, at the entrance of the Golden Horn. . . . The camera itself moves widely over the landscape, taking in the customers and the tables but also the many mosques with their minarets rising up in the distance, the Galata Bridge and the little ferries moving in every direction.

As a background to the images, there are nondialogue, real sounds: a woman's voice singing, a scream, car noises, boat noises, work noises, party noises, barking dogs, sea noises, musical instrument sounds. They either increase the realism of the atmosphere or introduce disturbing elements.

Sometimes the sounds harmonize with the sights realistically, such as the clinking glasses' sound and the laughter at the party, but sometimes they provide an indefinable atmosphere that is not

3 / THE HIDDEN *I* AND THE CAMERA EYE

wholly realistic but is right for the setting, such as the music of the flute and the saxophone and the woman's singing during the scenes on the streets of Istanbul. Sometimes they recur out of context as foreboding signs of future events, such as the barking of the dogs during otherwise peaceful scenes.

Michel Fano was Robbe-Grillet's executive producer and sound maker for *L'Immortelle* and later films. He explains the organization of sound in Robbe-Grillet's films by what he calls "musical order."[7]

> [Musical order is] a complex of relations in which the same form can be applied to diverse matters, in order to bring together objects of different natures with the only condition being that these objects respect among themselves the same relations as those formulations between the symbols not defined by the theory.... Musical Order is, before everything, the distribution of energy in the functioning of time; that is to say, the organization of pitches, or timbres, of intensities in the function of duration. (173)

When the images and the sounds of the film are examined side by side, the subtleties in the distribution of pitches and in the exchange of energy or intensity become clearer. For one, the selection of sounds and the timing of the sounds with each other and with the images make an ordinary situation or action seem ominous:

Shots 4 through 11 (pages 13–18):

Image	Sound
Shot 4 opens as the slats of a blind (a jalousie) open up; L's face is in close-up, without being blocked by the blind; the screen suddenly goes black.	The sound of a motor boat is heard as it recedes; Turkish music played on an alto sax is heard.
Shots 5, 6, 7, 8, and 9 are of the same duration—brief and fading rapidly, each shot replacing the previous one immediately; the camera is stationary and the figure of L in all the shots is also motionless.	The Turkish music on the alto sax continues; the deep barking of dogs continues through 7, 8, and 9; in 9, the engine of a fishing boat starts up.

In Shot 10, L is in the same position as in 9, but she is in another place; the shot includes all of L and some of the room. The camera is stationary, but L moves around to face the camera; then the camera moves until she is in closeup, the slats appear over her face and they close, until the screen is black.	A chugging motor boat is heard; the dogs are barking violently.
Shot 11 is a repetition of Shot 3; N is standing at the window; at first, he is stationary; then he raises his hand to open the slats. The shot changes when the blinds are open.	The sound of the motor boat dies away; another begins and increases in volume.

The opening and the closing of the blinds in several of these shots reveal the characters and then hide them. The characters are either immobile or slow moving in all the shots; as a counterpoint to this repetition and lack of action, the barking is violent. The motor boat and the saxophone alternate as melody or staccato beat. The short shots involving L (5 through 9) are linked by the music. The timbre of sounds varies: melody, staccato motors, harsh barking.

In shots 162 through 170 (pages 104–7), N is interviewing several men to get information about L. Each shot is an alternating closeup of N or of one of the men. The shots are cut abruptly. The sounds in the background are indistinct and varied: conversation, prayers in Turkish by one or several voices. The men have foreign accents and are contradictory in their information. The total effect is confusion and a feeling of alienation for both N and the audience.

The sequence of shots 233 through 253 (pages 130–35) combines a variety of images and a few sounds. The past is being relived:

3 / THE HIDDEN *I* AND THE CAMERA EYE

Image	Sound
The camera moves from one side of the police station room to the other; it passes over the motionless faces of the police in the room; the movement stops with a closeup of N, in a vaguely defined background. There is a cut to N's drawing room, a counter-shot from the door towards the windows; the camera advances toward the window and the sea outside the window takes over the entire frame.	A motor launch is heard, and the sound continues for several shots; the siren of a steamer concludes the series of shots made by the moving camera.
The camera cuts to the deck of the ferryboat, with L centered against the rail; the shot is stationary and L is stationary but the background is moving and changing. The shot continues stationary as the boat moves to the right, seemingly closer to the shore.	The chugging of the motor launch increases in volume and passes.
The camera cuts to the dunes, with L positioned as in Shot 8; she is motionless but begins a movement with her arm.	
The camera cuts to the interior of the car, which is moving, with rows of trees passing on each side.	The sound of the car engine can be heard.
The camera cuts to L at the wheel of the car with N beside her; N moves his hand toward the wheel; the shot is brief.	There is a sound of squealing tires and then of a collision.
The camera cuts to the woman standing in the dunes, completing the raising of her arm and turning toward the camera. The shot is very brief, like the preceding one.	

The camera cuts to the dog in front of the car; the dog is in closeup; the shot is briefer than the preceding one.	The shot ends with the sounds of the collision.

The sequence of shots 233 through 253 has ended with a minor climax that is not fully explained and, in fact, is further confused in meaning by the next sequence, a series of disconnected images beginning with N's face: the road moving past the car faster and faster; N in his room in front of a large mirror, his arm moving and his fingers making a stroking gesture like the one that he had previously made on L's face; a decorative detail of two bulging roses on a table leg; L walking toward the camera, near the water, but because of the lens used in the camera, always appearing to be the same distance away from the viewer; L at the wheel of the car; the interior of the car, as it moves rapidly down the road. The last shot is only a few frames in duration, and then the camera focusses on the sign YAVAS, toward which the dollying camera then moves rapidly until the sign is entirely in closeup, followed by a closeup of N's face, which ends when he turns his face quickly. During all these shots, a woman's voice is singing, the same voice heard at the beginning of the film.

At the end of that sequence, there is a shot of a doorknob advancing rapidly toward the viewer (another illusion of a moving camera), at the same time that the singing continues but is now accompanied by sounds of the accident—a scream, squealing tires, but not the collision sound itself. Finally, N is shown standing in front of the mirror with the doorknob in view because of the angle of the shot; he is staring at the knob and then he looks up at his reflection. The singing dies down; L's laughter is heard.

The sound of the motor launch begins again and L's voice is heard: "All this is a product of your imagination."

The sequence begins and ends with shots of N's face, suggesting that what is contained is in the narrator's head, reliving the events of the accident and his involvement in it, his obsession with certain details connected with the accident and with his experience of his room and its decorative elements. Obsession is suggested particularly by focussing on images that do not come closer (L near the water) and the camera's closing in on images (the sign and the doorknob).

3 / THE HIDDEN *I* AND THE CAMERA EYE

The singing is a continuous rhythm that links alternating slow and rapid shots, in which the protagonists are motionless but the objects and the camera are hurried. L's comment at the end of the sequence reminds the viewer that his/her mind and imagination—all in the head—are susceptible to suggestion and manipulation. Another sequence plays with the relationship between real and imagined—shots 43–48 (pages 39–43)—as N and L take the ferry down the Bosphorus. The real places being photographed are seen by them and are commented on by L, either in direct conversation with N or in a voice-over:

Look, there is the mosque of your dreams.[8]

All this is a product of your imagination. . . . You see . . . you are on the Bosphorus. You are skirting the coast of Asia. . . . Below the minarets you can see the wooden houses with closed windows, where women are shut away. (40)

Look, those boats are not what they seem. . . . They're bringing women prisoners back as slaves. (41)

And to enter the palaces of your sleepless nights, the fragile constructions by the water's edge, the magical East of the picture postcards, stucco facades, decorations painted in trompe-l'oeil on stretched canvases all around your room. . . . Do you recognize them? The columns and porticos. (43)

By such comments, L suggests to N and to the audience that dreams and fantasies about real places color and distort their perceptions, and illusions and imitations of the real image fill their heads and their imaginations. The heroine, L, may be an illusion and is certainly full of contradictions: she denies knowing the fat man, though she is seen next to him several times; people speak Turkish to her, but she claims she does not understand it; she says she is French but later will not tell what her nationality is; her name may be Leila, Lâle, Eliane, or Lucille. The film is full of real images and real sounds, but the images are either hiding true situations or are pretending to be mysterious, and the sounds are used as accompaniment, as forewarning, or to help create a climax in the action.

The camera is the narrative eye, more knowledgeable than the human narrator N: it describes by showing; it gives impressions and suggests moods and meanings. A number of conventional film techniques are used to produce description and alert imagination: a tracking (or dollying) or panning camera imitates eye or head movements; freeze frames give an impression that an image should be remembered; high angle shots show a dissociation from the subject; closeups indicate an intensity of impression; depth-of-field shots try to clarify all the events and details in the frame; images are centered in the frame to focus attention on them in a particular context.[9]

The opening shot of the film is a tracking shot of the walls of Constantinople (Istanbul), which is concluded by sounds that do not belong to that time and place—screeching brakes and tires, a scream, a crash. The traveling camera thus introduces the viewer to Istanbul, to a narrative eye, and to a premonition of future events. When the same shot is repeated using the same details, the shot is remembered by the audience, and perhaps by the protagonist-narrator. The eye and the mind are joined, as images move in and out of our minds quickly.

A tracking shot can also suggest movement in time as the camera moves in space, such as the shot at the party that spots Leila and N in one corner of the room and then travels in a rapid panning movement across the room and spots them in front of the window. They have moved, but not as fast as the camera has; the rapid movement of the camera is a shorthand form of suggesting a continuity in time, signaled by a camera movement; in novels, phrases like "one hour later" perform a similar function. The shorthand action of the camera—either by such rapid tracking or panning or by abrupt cutting—makes the camera a very active participant in the narrative.

In another scene, the movement of the camera in one environmental context, a garden, indicates a passage of time as well as the slowing down of time for two people who want to be with each other. In several shots, as the camera first picks out the protagonists and then passes them by, they become incidental to the camera eye's leisurely movement:

3 / THE HIDDEN *I* AND THE CAMERA EYE

Shot 79, pages 63–64
: The movement of the filming apparatus—a slow and regular rotation, from left to right—goes forward without pausing over the characters more than over the rest of the scene. N, who is looking at L, lying down near him, turns slowly toward the right of the screen of which he occupies the center, looking beyond the field, in the direction toward which the camera continues to pivot, as though to show what he is seeing. The shot is cut when N is on the left third of the screen.

The next two shots continue the movement, first picking out and then passing by the characters. By means of this casual movement, the camera and the audience for whom it is playing are freed for the moment from the domination of plot and character. The characters seem to be there accidentally.

On the other hand, a passive (not moving) camera allows itself to be dominated for the sake of absorbing the external but suggestive elements of a place or a character. Prolonged closeups, the most obvious form of camera passivity, demand that the audience pay attention as the camera reduces its role in the action. During closeups, the slightest movement of the character becomes important and must be observed; in the frequent closeups of characters in *L'Immortelle*, the faces are generally impassive, except for a slight smile, a strange look in the eyes, a blink.

Sometimes the impassivity becomes deliberately staged immobility: the men sitting in the background at the café where N talks to Catherine Sarayan; the workmen at the ruins of Byzantium, where L and N part; the guests at N's party. Since a sense of moving life is expected in a film image, immobility and posing are very unlifelike. Freeze frames (in which there is no camera movement and which catch the image and hold it as though it were a photograph) are extreme ways of pointing out a significance in the caught pose or expression. By being passive or by holding the image passive, the camera is forcing attention on an object or situation that might otherwise be forgotten or ignored. When a camera behaves in an abnormal way (prolonged immobility or fast panning movement), it is describing and suggesting by gesture.

Editing is a very important part of the filmmaking process, giving a film its rhythm and tempo, introducing elements that oppose the effects of realism by special effects. In *L'Immortelle*, symbols are created by the use of special effects. A number of shots produce images that cannot be realistic but seem significant and "real" to the characters: in a dusky part of the mosque, after L's death, N sees L's image fading in and out (shots 284–88, pages 146–47); in a series of photographs that N examines, L does not appear in the first nine photos of the same shot but does appear in the last ten of the identical shot (shot 291, pages 148–49); in the last shot of the film (shot 355, page 173), the "dead" L is on the deck of the ferry, looking at the audience and laughing.

These moments are "real" either to the narrator-protagonist or to the audience; they are the camera/editing method of imitating the action of the mind. Inner reality is being shown; it can be seen. In the film, the way the mind works is much more important than the truth or falsity of the events. How can the truth or falsity of the action be explained since the motivations of the characters are mysterious, ambiguous, or insubstantial? The camera eye does not help to explain the action, but it can be a convincing tool of mental action. Confusions and delusions of mental reality are not questioned. N remains the narrator and point of view of the film, though this role is challenged at the end of the film, when the images continue after N's death.

The Narrator and the Point of View

The narrator N tells the story (through his eye rather than through speech) in three cycles of action. The first cycle is the seemingly realistic plot based on place, characters, a mystery, and a death. Disturbing elements are introduced in this cycle, but they do not impede the action. The ironic counterpoint to the perceived (eye) action is mythological, popular fantasy belief, such as expressed by Catherine Sarayan as she talks to N in a café: "Kidnappings, secret prisons, girls sold as slaves . . . and all kinds of strange trafficking . . . on behalf of foreign countries" (shots 260–63, pages 138–39).

3 / THE HIDDEN *I* AND THE CAMERA EYE

Catherine's expression is (in the ciné-roman's words) "earnest, visionary, exaggerated," and, though these popular fantasies are being mocked, N, the professor, finds it hard not to believe her, since L has disappeared.

The second cycle stresses the emotional tone, particularly N's emotional state. In the first cycle, he has seemed uncertain and uneasy; as images and events are repeated in his memory during the second cycle, his anxiety becomes obsession. His search for L heightens his suspicions and his obsession.

The third cycle, which begins after L's death, shows the narrator's distorted memory and fantasy. L is remembered in images that show fear, mockery, or sensuality. N remembers certain scenes repeatedly; these memories are part of his obsessive attempt to recapture their experiences together and to examine his guilt or innocence for her death. This cycle concludes with what may be a self-execution. Each part is like a movement in a symphony. In the first movement, the central character, or observer, is quiet and neutral. He moves slowly and shows little expression. As L provokes him, he becomes bolder, making comments such as "I shall have to beat you" (shot 88, page 71). Other movements begin to show a restrained violence. In shot 71, page 60, he puts his hand on her neck, and in shot 83, page 68, L responds to his touch fearfully:

> Just as N is about to touch L, she lowers her arms and looks up; there is an expression of fear in her eyes. She moves her head quickly to right and left, as if she is trying to escape but is tied to the spot.

The camera movements and N's body and eye movements mostly coincide during this part.

In the second movement, the search, he is still neutral as he responds to the people he meets. But he shows signs of suspicion and confusion, and the audience shares his confusion. Through the medium of the camera, acting like his eye, the audience sees actions in a new and suspicious light: a curtain in a window is lifted and dropped when the camera eye spies it; the fisherman on the quay seems to be spying on him. Spying, searching, and suspecting are the themes of the action, and the audience is dominated by the interpretations of N the observer.

In the third movement, after L's accident, the experiences that N remembers are different from the experiences that the audience has seen in the first movement of the film. N's fantasies have become his reality, and he is no longer a reliable observer of events or an objective interpreter of memories. The audience is made aware of this translation of memory in a number of shots.

In shot 257, pages 136–37, when N remembers the conversation on the beach, he adds a comment he did not make in the original scene: "Who was that man with dark glasses who was with you when I first met you? Was he your father?"

In shot 263, page 139, M (the husband-father?) is shown in closeup, and now N remembers him as sitting in the café with his dogs, who are growling threateningly. In the next shot, L appears, and she has a conversation with M that had not taken place in the original scene (shot 42, pages 37–38). In shot 266, page 140, N now remembers a "heated dialogue of which not a word can be heard because of the ship's sirens."

In shot 288, page 147, L reveals fears which she had never expressed before:

N: Are you afraid of being watched?

L: Of course not. . . . I'm not afraid. . . . I am free.

Her protests and her tone of voice are anxious and tense.

In shots 301–6, pages 152–54, L's poses are more erotic than in earlier scenes. The chain she has been wearing casually as a belt and a necklace is now thrown across her neck and chest like a chain of enslavement.

N's hallucinations about L (as he imagines her appearance and disappearance in the mosque or in the photographs) confirm the fact that for him reality has become completely subjective. As he drives the car, he seems to be in a hypnotic state. The dog in the road may be real or it may be a fantasy; it becomes an excuse to destroy himself. The final images of the film reveal his state of mind and the distorted, objective reality we see:

3 / THE HIDDEN *I* AND THE CAMERA EYE

Shots 342–55 (pages 169–73):

Image	Sound
As in Shot 1, the ancient walls of Constantinople are shown through the interior of a car which is in motion; the light indicates it is approaching dusk.	The woman singer begins her song. L's voice is heard: "The ramparts of Byzantium. . . . They are having to be rebuilt once more. . . . From the Sea of Marmora to the Golden Horn, as far as the eye can see, you pass a succession of ruined Towers . . . to the castle of the Seven Prisons. . . . But you go where the mood takes you. . . . You are a foreigner here. . . . You have arrived in the Turkey of your dreams. . . . Spurious prisons, spurious ramparts, spurious stories. . . . You cannot go back.
A car is seen in a long shot moving along the road and it exits front left. The road is seen through the windshield of the previous interior, N at the wheel. Through the windshield, M appears holding one of his dogs and watches without moving.	L's voice continues, "Let's go further out. I'll explain."

L's voice says, "Further on . . . You saw that." |
| The road seen through the windshield is the one seen earlier, with the trees and the signposts. | The singing voice continues; it becomes more agitated. L's voice says, "We must go on. . . . Faster. . . . Oh, it's too difficult." L's voice says, "You're wrong. There was no one with me. . . . Faster." |
| There is a counter-shot of N at the wheel, full face, looking at the camera, seeming to look at the road. It is a closeup; the movement of the car is not obvious. | |

The camera cuts to a position behind N, the road outside visible. The dog appears in the light of the headlights.	The singing continues.
N's face is seen full face in closeup, with a fixed expression. The expression and the shot are unmoving.	
The camera cuts to a closeup of the dog's head and upper body. An optical effect makes the body larger than possible until his head fills the screen.	L's screams from the first accident are heard, as are the squealing tires.
N's face is seen enlarged in closeup; it is a brief shot.	The squealing of the brakes and the tires continues.
The camera cuts to the large head of the dog, which occupies the whole screen. He opens his jaws to bark. The screen goes dark.	At the end of the shot, the collision sounds are heard.
There is a complete darkness for a few seconds. Then the picture brightens and N is seen in the same position as L when she was killed; his head has fallen to one side, toward the camera. His eyes are open.	There is a sound of crickets, as after the first accident.
N's face is seen in closeup.	The sound of the crickets continues at varying volumes.
The camera cuts to L's face as she reclines on cushions on the divan, as in Shot 2. The bright picture becomes blurred.	The cricket sounds continue. They are replaced by ship's sirens.

3 / THE HIDDEN *I* AND THE CAMERA EYE

The camera cuts to a very dark exterior shot. L's image is clear as she stands on the prow of the ferry. The mosques in the background gradually gets closer, as the boat moves. She bursts into silent laughter. Then her face becomes immobile. The credits cover her image.	The sounds of the sirens continue, accompanied by rhythmic hammer strokes. A sad song, heard earlier in Shot 321, is heard again.

As N drives the car, his memories overwhelm his senses. The sounds and images repeat the pattern that was initiated in the beginning sequences of the film. The movement of the film has been generated, and the generation is developed by Robbe-Grillet's form of metaphor—metonymy. Objects and events change their forms, always suggesting links to the originating form. One example that catches and focuses the erotic nature of the film—without any sex scenes—is the dance of the belly dancer in the middle of the film. It is watched attentively by an audience of men and by N and L and sensually pictorializes N's feelings toward L—sexual with an undertone of violence. This sexual/violent attitude toward women is particularly related to that place—Istanbul—and to an embodiment of the female image that Robbe-Grillet uses in other works: the sorceress motif. This image was possibly borrowed from Jules Michelet's (1798–1874) study *La Sorcière*[10] and is an acknowledged generator of the film *Glissements progressifs du plaisir* (1974), in the character of Alice.[11] However, Alice is a free spirit, according to Robbe-Grillet, whom society is trying to suppress, whereas Lâle is an almost passive victim of her society. Lâle is one metonymic version of the sorceress image, and she reflects Robbe-Grillet's own expression of freedom; he will not be held to one version of an original idea.

Robbe-Grillet is a *transformer* of ideas and processes of writing. He does not hold himself to a set of philosophical or aesthetic beliefs (admittedly a slippery way of conducting himself creatively) and is far more interested in following his own pathways as they are suggested—generated—by a variety of sources.

The gaze of the narrator, N, in *L'Immortelle* is the camera eye, lured in its perceptions to seeing people and things in confusing and increasingly obsessional ways. Voices and sounds direct or reflect the states of mind of N and the audience. Repetition with variation alerts the audience to states of mind, and the subtle variations in movement, from perception of real images to fantasizing through memory and imagination, are held together by the repetition. Repetition is done in the film according to an internally detectable tempo; though the connection of images and sounds seems to be erratic, there is a pattern of alternation between static images and rapid editing. It may be a rhythm close to an audience's rhythms of attention. Sometimes an action is boring, and sometimes it is exciting, perhaps as Robbe-Grillet projects his own patterns of attention.

The labyrinth is another way of describing the generated pattern of action in Robbe-Grillet's works, particularly illustrated in the novel *In the Labyrinth* (1960). The gaze in this novel is very unobtrusive, confined to an "I" at the beginning, to a "you" in one description of walking in the snow, to words like "maybe, might be, probably, gives the impression," to the return of "I" as a doctor, and to the final word of the book "behind me." The action of the novel is defined by the soldier's arrivals at various places—once? twice? three times?—the street corner, the apartment of the woman who may be the child's mother, the café-bar, the barracks-hospital. The final exit from the novel is his death. The soldier's purported purpose—to deliver a box (described in different ways at different times) to someone—is never actually accomplished, though a box is examined by various strangers.

What is labyrinthine in this novel is superficially related to the physical wanderings of the soldier, his return more than once to places that should be landmarks but aren't. Another labyrinthine relation is to the confusions and blocked thought passages in the soldier's head so that he cannot seem to find the right route or even his own purpose in looking for his destination. But he won't give up. Perhaps unlike the obsessed, exploring narrator in *L'Immortelle*, he does not imagine the worst, although he wonders about a man with crutches who appears in different places as the soldier appears there, but he doesn't wonder very much. His

3 / THE HIDDEN *I* AND THE CAMERA EYE

obsessive quest—only obsessive because he persists in spite of pain—is almost somnolent, only occasionally dreamlike. His labyrinth is a trap, from which he can be released only by death—and perhaps that is the whole "story." Nevertheless, Robbe-Grillet cannot help but evoke atmospheres—like the atmosphere of anxiety in *The Erasers*—and the atmosphere of *In the Labyrinth* is one of defeat, the defeat of the soldier's army at "Reichenfels." The town seems to be anticipating its occupation by enemy forces, but with resignation, not hysteria. The labyrinth idea includes a sense of hopelessness, of a cycle of endless and useless repetition of actions, with only a scant hope of release. But all these ideas about *labyrinth* are subjective ideas, related to internal feelings and moods. Whose internal feelings? The "I" narrator has set a scene and a form of exterior/interior in the descriptions at the beginning of the novel; the soldier, once introduced, through his confused and half-remembered purposes establishes the meandering route that becomes the form of the novel; the reader becomes involved in the hopelessness of the action. The writer, in his guise as I-doctor, perhaps, but certainly in a recording gaze that follows the soldier from scene to scene, is unobtrusively present and unobtrusively establishes the feeling of the work.

Stephen Heath defines *In the Labyrinth* as "the action of the narrative taking possession of itself.... *Dans le Labyrinth* is not a novel in the conventional sense which defines an area of expectation (story, character, in short, Sense), but a handful of novelistic fragments ... and the 'subject' of the book is not in the conventional sense of these fragments, but in their ... exploration as *forms* in the text ... to *read* a Robbe-Grillet text ... [is] to respond to the activity of the text, to its construction."[12]

Nevertheless, as the reader is drawn into the reading by responding to its construction, the sense (feeling) of the text emerges. Everything described is subjectified, made significant or insignificant by the form of its description.

An interesting way that Robbe-Grillet creates a feeling of subjectivity is through the use of the "impersonal" definite article *the* (*le* or *la*) when referring to objects and to body parts, particularly to *the* eye. *The* should create a feeling of flatness, of objective description, but instead it focusses the attention of the reader on the body part and makes that part significant. *The eye* becomes the *only* eye; almost the whole novel *Jealousy* is dominated by the use of *the*, particularly *the eye*.

Jealousy, or *La Jalousie* (with its double meaning in French of an emotion and a window blind) was written before *In the Labyrinth*, or *L'Immortelle*. The narrator as an "I" or as a description or as observed by anyone else never appears in the narrative except as a third place set at the table for the almost daily dinners with the neighbor Franck. Yet *the eye* of the narrator constantly observes, spies, measures, and eventually speculates and imagines what it does not observe (or presumably a mind behind the eye performs these functions).

The feeling projected in the novel is strongly one of obsession and finally barely restrained violence, culminating in the imaginary (one assumes) vision of an automobile crashing and going up in flames. This climactic moment is referred to only once in the novel, after which the narrative continues as it had, with repetitions of scenes and explanations; the explanations relate to the overnight stay in town of the wife and the neighbor because of engine trouble, they said.

The audience can see and hear the narrator in *L'Immortelle*, though his blankness of expression prevents sympathy; the reader can hardly identify the narrators of *In the Labyrinth* and *Jealousy* but becomes enclosed in the labyrinthine spaces in which they seem to be confined and into which the reader is trapped. The narrators stand in for the author, who maintains his distance from the readers/audience but manipulates them and guides them and must convince them that they are not going to reach a resolution; they must be satisfied with the ambiguous conclusions of the actions (though death, for whatever reason and whatever cause, is fairly conclusive, and two of the narrators or central protagonists do die).

In these works, Robbe-Grillet has transformed almost all the conventional elements of novels and films. Movements of camera and language replace cause and effect; story is doubled and mixed up chronologically by the time shifts; the character of characters cannot be pinned down; spaces and routes replace landscape and setting; and the author creates the impression that he has no moral or meaning in mind.

There are other ways of confusing meaning, and the next two works are examples of those techniques of narration and description.

4
Perception and Deception: *The Man Who Lies* and *Djinn*

Lying as a method of narration structures and deconstructs the film *The Man Who Lies* and the novel *Djinn*. In both works, following circular routes directed by many generators and motifs, words and images in both the novel and the film confuse and manipulate readers and viewers, involving them in games of perception and deception. *The Man Who Lies* was produced in 1968 (Robbe-Grillet's third film) as a joint French-Czechoslovakian enterprise, and *Djinn* was published in 1982, originally at the request of a department of French language. There is no relationship between them in terms of plot. But parody and game playing with plot and myth overtly challenge readers and viewers to examine the nature of reality and to follow unique organizational patterns.

The Man Who Lies seems to be flirting with social comment. What are heroes? When might heroes become traitors? Why does Robbe-Grillet use a war and postwar environment? Only one tentative explanation emerges from the questions raised: heroes and wars are facts of life that can be used as generating images. Like the other realities that Robbe-Grillet uses (artworks, places, and popular images), historical and mythical-historical situations are rich sources for the generation of images and motifs. And, as he did in *L'Immortelle*, he has used audience gullibility about the believability of film images as a challenge; many of this film's images and stories test credibility. Like *L'Immortelle*, *The Man Who Lies* is divided into movements and variations on movements, and

4 / PERCEPTION AND DECEPTION

it is accompanied by a musical score that accentuates the actions in the film but also has a life of its own.

At the film's opening, a man in civilian clothes is being pursued by soldiers in a forest. There is a lot of machine-gun fire, and finally the man falls down. However, the next morning he gets up from the ground, brushes himself off, and begins to walk. As he is walking, a voice-over begins to tell his story, which even during this telling is changed and modified several times as he walks and as he enters a village. In a café, he overhears many admiring comments about a Jean Robin and other comments about some women who live in a chateau outside of town. He finds the chateau[1] and makes advances to each of the women, who turn out to be Jean Robin's wife, his sister, and a maid who has never seen Jean.

He is successful with the maid, Maria, and with the sister, Sylvie, but is resisted by the wife, Laura. He tells them all that he was an intimate friend of Jean's and was his companion during the Resistance, and he tells stories to illustrate their friendship. When he is questioned, he either hedges or changes his story.

Jean's father and his manservant live at the chateau too. First they ignore the man (whose name is given as Boris), but then they expel him from the house after he sleeps with the maid. They do not believe his stories about Jean.

In the village, he becomes friendly with the maid at the café, which is also an inn where he gets a room. He also visits the pharmacy, about which he is told a story having to do with some German soldiers and Jean's activities during the Resistance. He later tells the same story with modifications, including himself in the action. The film images that illustrate *his* version, which includes himself, show the woman at the pharmacy betraying Jean and Boris to the Germans. He tells other stories about *Jean's* betrayal of his comrades and about *his* (Boris's) own execution by the Underground as a traitor.

Jean's father is killed in what may be an accident or may be murder by the manservant. Boris moves into the chateau and tries to command and dominate the women. He is haunted by memories and dreams of pursuit. During a sequence in which he tries to force the wife, Laura, to sleep with him, they are suddenly confronted by the living presence of Jean, who has presumably returned from hiding. Boris is shot by Jean, but when everyone leaves, Boris gets up from the floor and begins to tell his story again. As he talks, his face changes into Jean's. In the last shots, Boris is running through the forest, pursued by the camera again. The music that accompanied the first images is heard again, but there is no shooting.

Camera Technique Questions Realism

The first shots of the film show a man running in a forest, occasionally looking behind him. The camera seems to be pursuing him. The images waver, as happens when a camera is handheld. The next shots show a number of soldiers coming through the forest too, firing at intervals. The soldiers and the man are not shown in the same frame. Both the pursuit and the firing are sporadic but seem realistic.

However, the scene is not realistic. The man is wearing a 1960s sport coat and a shirt and tie, and the soldiers are wearing World War II helmets. Occasionally, machine guns and hand grenades are used, but though the man falls down frequently, he always rises and continues on his way. Several times he pauses and looks back, and once he climbs a tree to look around. Since there is very little tension and no one is hurt, the relationship between the pursuers and the pursued has elements of a game.

Finally, after a burst of gunfire, the man falls down in some bushes, making extravagant gestures as though he has been hit. As he lies there, the light on the screen fades and then gradually brightens, as though day were breaking. The man stirs and sits up. No one has approached him as he lay motionless; he does not seem to expect anyone when he gets up.

The whole preceding sequence is put in question: was it a dream, a fantasy, or fragmented reality?

In retrospect, the sounds have been too isolated and unnaturally loud. Many minor sounds, like panting breath and running feet, have been heard very distinctly in spite of the loud gun shots and the explosions. The noises were accompanied by musical

4 / PERCEPTION AND DECEPTION

sounds; crashing chords and plucking strings and the ratatatat of drums has alternated with the natural sounds. Michel Fano, the associate producer of the film and the sound engineer, explains the use of the sounds:

> It would be a question here of a sort of thematic overture, that is to say an introduction to the sound themes of the film.[2]

When the man falls down, the sounds cease, but they begin again when he awakens, and they recur all through the first reel. The musical chords and beats are heard alone, without the gunfire. Although the connections between sound and image and between the alternating kinds of shots (closeups, long shots, mid-shots) seem arbitrary, they all constitute what Robbe-Grillet calls a "concrete music":[3]

> Everything together (the montage, the route, the appearance of the images, the noise) must give the impression of an obsessive race, of broken rhythms, of ineluctable accelerations. (138)

The camera's point of view is not clearly controlled. First it follows the man; then it shows individual soldiers in closeup. Then the man is shown in a long shot when he falls into the bushes. Sometimes the camera is active, sometimes passive; sometimes it is steady, sometimes agitated. The editing too emphasizes the ambiguity of all the relationships. The man and his pursuers are never shown in the same frame, but they are assumed to be reacting to each other because of the alternative cutting between them and because they are in the same setting. The duration of the shots varies, like the jumpy rhythms of the sound effects. After the man awakens, a voice-over begins to tell his story. Voice-overs are conventionally used to express the thoughts of a character or are used when a story is being remembered. In a travelogue, they comment on or explain the scene. In this film, the voice-over tells a story by inventing the characters and events, sometimes in relation to the settings and sometimes in contradiction to the images we see:

> My name is Robin . . . Jean Robin. . . . I am going to tell you my story . . . or, at least, I am going to try. (Brief silence)

> Here it is: it all began in a forest, a big forest.... There was a sort of path not clearly marked.... [P]reviously, there had been a brook, a stone in the running water ... some dead branches.
>
> But no ... it was rather a field, a large field without a fence with thistle seeds that blew in the wind ... (a silence) ... without doubt in the proximity of a small city or a large village.
>
> Where was I? ... Oh yes! My name is Boris.... But in general the others call me Jean ... and sometimes the Ukranian, I have never known why.... (There is a silence.) I'll begin again. The first time that I arrived at the village, I wandered at first around the streets, anonymous among the crowds of passersby (there is a scene of Boris wandering in a deserted street).... Jean ... of course, I must speak of Jean.... He was my friend, my comrade, my fighting companion.... Yes, the streets were deserted, evidently. It was during the war, and the people went out of their houses as little as possible; they did not much like consorting with the occupation troops, nor showing their papers ten times a day to enemy soldiers or to the civilian guards, who patrolled two by two all the crossroads.... Yes, that's it ... the grazing horses and the sentinels that swarmed at the corners of the streets.... I don't remember whether I have already told the story of the woman in the pharmacy and of the inspection roadblock that they raised across the road, at the entrance of the town.... (pause) The first time, then, that I arrived in the village, I was directed to the right towards the inn, empty also, as was usual at this morning hour ...(the noise of the inn full of people, in flagrant contradiction to his words, ought to be inserted in the cut at the moment that Boris turns toward the door ...) (143–44)

There is a trial-and-error method in the storytelling. After describing the streets as crowded, Boris redescribes them as deserted "evidently." The evidence is in the image we have been shown, in which he is alone on the street. He elaborates on the image of the deserted streets by explaining the time and place of the event. But this explanation is contradicted by the noisy crowd in the inn, who should be home rather than in a public place at that time of day.

The man tries to establish his identify by three shifts of focus. First he is Jean Robin; then he is Jean Robin called Boris or the Ukranian. Then he is Boris, whose close friend is Jean. This uncertain identity will be reflected later in the imagery: the two characters Boris and Jean resemble each other.

Interrupting the flow of the imagery and the sound of the voice-over are contamination shots, each shot longer than the previous one, of three women. First there is a brief shot of Laura (the wife) tossing her hair, then a later shot of Laura laughing. There is a shot of the three women playing blind man's buff, then later shots of the game in more detail. There are long shots of the halls and stairways of the house in which they are playing the game. As the shots get longer, the scene establishes itself as a parallel story. The game of blind man's buff is, as Tom Bishop has suggested, also a metaphor for the trial-and-error technique of this tale.[4] In addition, he says, it is a "sign of the eroticism of the relations between the characters" (62).

There are many other false starts in the film, particularly in the parallel but opposing stories that are told. Two stories are each told more than once. Each story concerns a hero who, in the second version of each story, is really a traitor. Boris tells both versions of the first story, and later he tells a revised version of another story told to him by the maid in the café.

The first version of the first story concerns an escape from a makeshift prison by Jean, with help from his Underground friends. In this version, Jean is taken by Boris to a safe place but is wounded on the way. Boris tells a second version to the maid, Maria, in the chateau, with Sylvie, Jean's sister, spying on them and overhearing the story. In this later version, Jean betrays his comrades when they come to rescue him.

The versions of the stories are changed according to the contexts in which they are told. The first version was told in the café where Jean is revered as a hero and where Boris keeps trying to ingratiate himself. The second version is told at the chateau, where Boris is trying to destroy the occupants' image of Jean in order to replace him. Later, his wish to replace Jean is stated explicitly. The trial-and-error method is a calculated trick, adding another complication to tale-telling in order to point out that the work is a fiction, an accepted fiction. Many people in the village, as well as Sylvie, were supposed to be involved in the stories of the escape, but nobody challenges either version.

The second story of betrayal is first told to Boris by the maid in the café and then is told by Boris to Sylvie. The maid's story is a heroic version of the involvement of Jean and the girl in the pharmacy in the Underground. Boris's version is generated by at least three factors: his desire to humiliate and seduce Sylvie, the maid's story, and a series of photos of Jean that Boris finds in a book in the pharmacy. The book is labeled *Codex* and, in the usual use of the term, should contain descriptions of prescriptions but instead is full of pictures of Jean at various stages of his life. The term *Codex* is being given another connotation: code book for Jean's life. The *Codex* is a form of *mise en abyme*, like the stories or images that appear in other Robbe-Grillet works and serve to condense the essential elements of each work, *but not to explain them*. Besides the storytelling methods described, there are dream and fantasy images that interrupt and parallel the action.

To the subjective consciousness, dreams and illusions are as real as objective experience. The phenomenologist Merleau-Ponty recognizes that appearance and reality are equally valid as experiences of the mind:

> It has often been said that consciousness, by definition, admits of no separation of appearance and reality, and by this we are to understand that, in our knowledge of ourselves, appearance is reality: if I think I see or feel, I indubitably see or feel, whatever may be true of the external object.[5]

From the moment that Boris leaps into the film frame in the first shots of the film, he is created for our immediate perception. Then, as he begins talking about himself, he creates more of himself, and every story thereafter adds to his history or to the myth of himself that he wants to have accepted. The-man-who-lies invents myths to add a reality to his appearance. His myth takes form because of a number of generators: past real history, present environment, the appearance of other characters, his growing ambition and desire, his dreams, and his fantasies. Jean Robin, as an ideal figure and as a photographed real figure (there are photographs of him everywhere that Boris looks, and he looks at them often), inspires Boris's imagination. His status as a Resistance hero invites parody. Boris mocks him, denigrates him, and imitates him. The barren, grim look of the village and of the people are further provocations for Boris to invent tales of betrayal and revenge. The women in the chateau provoke him erotically and incite ambitions of control and authority.

Generators Direct the Artist's Imagination

As a filmmaker, Robbe-Grillet's imagination was inspired, first, by a place:

> [T]he forest was the material origin of the project: it was while crossing the immense forests of the eastern Carpathians ... that I had a desire to make a film. ... In this space of no man's land, there were only the vertical trunks of trees, then soldiers, then the shots, then a person who comes out of the bushes and who comes from nowhere.[6]

The forest appears in the first shots of the film, and the man disappears into the forest in the last shots. It provides the framework for the composition. The first shots use the contrasting elements of the rigid trees, the running people, and the wavering, hand-held camera. The metaphor of no-man's-land—used to describe the battlefields of World War I—is made real by the soldiers. They are making this no-man's-land a minor battlefield. The man's presence or connection to the battlefield is never explained, but he is literally thrown into the frame, and the action and is born at that moment; he develops his persona afterwards.

Another place also inspired Robbe-Grillet:

> At the base of *The Man Who Lies*, there is a house, a sort of half-ruined chateau, where the placement of rooms, corridors, entryways and stairs gives rise to a problematic idea of routes. It is a labyrinth, an archetype of labyrinth, but more than that, there is a presence, a materiality of decayed walls, of empty rooms, of attics cluttered with discarded objects, of cellars, etc., that constitute at the same time something solid as well as a sort of haunted domain, a residence of ghosts. It was very important for me to create in this domain variable and aleatory progressions. I don't know why, I can't find the adjective to characterize the signification of each of the routes, to say whether

> this is more rational, this crazier.... I have the impression, however, that each character must invent his own route, exactly as the reading of a film must be re-done by each spectator. The film is a haunted place, exactly as the house is a haunted place, in which one makes the film, and the journeyings of the actor in that place are comparable to the journeyings of the spectator.[7]

Almost the whole structure of the film is explained in this passage. The key words are *route, labyrinth, presence, progression,* and *haunted*. Though Robbe-Grillet says he is not prepared to discuss the "signification" of each route in explaining the characters, the journeyings (*parcours*) of the characters reflect the progress of the action in the film.

As noted previously, labyrinths have a meaning for Robbe-Grillet as symbols of the architectural confusions and hidden dangers of our lives. Whether the characters actually reveal themselves by their routes or whether Robbe-Grillet's personal fascination with meandering movement is the reason for following their movements through the house, movement of either camera or character is part of the rhythm of the film and creates its circular pattern. As one example, Sylvie's journey through the house as she goes to the attic in one episode is circuitous. She goes up some stairs, down corridors, up a ladder, and finally up a curving spiral staircase. She ascends by every possible upward movement available to the house. The house is full of climbing and connecting parts and of alcoves and corner angles, behind which Sylvie and Laura either spy or hide. Laura is often framed in arched doorways or is followed by the camera through crowded rooms. The clutter in many of the rooms constricts the space and makes the passageways narrow and winding. Robbe-Grillet worked with the cameraman to exploit these architectural elements:

> I said to Igor Luther, for *The Man Who Lies* or for *Eden*: what are the movements of the camera that you want to make in this ensemble of rooms? And it was, sometimes, by the functioning of the movements of the camera that he wanted to make, that is to say the creation of a route in the place in question, that I organized my scene. I have just pronounced the key word: a *route*; it happens that in the novels or the films the notion of route or journey is extremely important for me,

4 / PERCEPTION AND DECEPTION

more than the notion of place. But, each place is precisely a special place for certain types of routes.[8]

The house is a labyrinth of spaces; it has no clear architectural pattern and it is full of traps. The relationships between the inhabitants are also labyrinthine—ambiguous and shifting. Is the maid the companion and also the lover of Sylvie? Their relationship is not explained. The shifting and ambiguous relationships are like the structure of the film, which is marked by frequent changes in direction. Myth and historical events are also generators for the action of the film, which then parodies the myths and events. Boris Varissa, the hero, is a fictional descendant of Boris Godunov, the usurper. He attempts to usurp Jean's place as hero, lover, husband, and master of the house. As a lover, he is also a descendant of Don Juan:

> Jean becomes the character that he has made up. To make up oneself: it is what every man does. Between the real and the imaginary.
>
> My character: at the same time Boris Goudounov [sic] the usurping tsar, Don Juan. The Don Juan of Kierkegaard: the usurper and the seducer. Kierkegaard pointed out that he was not interested in seducing a young woman unless she was in love with another man. It was necessary that there be someone to drive away and to replace.[9]

Boris acts out the part of usurper and seducer, but occasionally he gives himself away as an actor. In one episode, he tells an obviously impossible story of his own execution by the Underground (enacting the event for Maria, who laughs at him). In another episode, he has a dream that is about the pursuit we saw at the beginning of the film, but there are dogs in this pursuit, and his fears are more obvious than they were at the beginning. The dream seems more real than the pursuit we thought was real. In the original pursuit, he seemed calm; as he is dreaming, he groans and tosses in the bed. Beneath the calm of his appearance, he is fearful. In another instance, he has a fantasy that Jean is pursuing him, and he backs off fearfully. When Laura observes him, he quickly recovers and makes up an excuse. In fact, he calls himself an actor. Appearance of calm and the reality of fear alternate and shift in his self-creation, and he is the link between the scenes in the episodic structure of the film. He either performs in every scene or listens to someone else's report of a past action. He either generates a story or responds to stories or questions from other characters. Each action or response encourages him to play a role. By his role playing, he participates in all the action. By his shifting versions of the stories, he confuses the action. He presents himself in different roles, often as a tactic for getting his own way, and sometimes that tactic includes admitting that he is role playing.

Just before he seduces Sylvie, he reads dramatically the lines from *Hamlet* "Doubt that the stars are fire," exaggerating his interest in her and making it artificial. When he is observed by Laura running from a ghost, he tells her, "I was putting on an act. I'm an actor." When he describes his execution to Maria, he dabs some mercurochrome on his shirt as though he were bleeding.

He is the role player and the writer—Robbe-Grillet himself, creating the narrative by a series of patterns, or motifs. There are four motifs, which are related to the action and atmosphere of the film. The action motifs are structural, since they involve repetitions and forms of linkage. The atmosphere motifs emphasize the slippery and ephemeral nature of the reality in the film.

Motif 1, *Flight*, begins with the pursuit of Boris through fields and woods by soldiers, which is recorded by a handheld camera. The wavering movements of the image, particularly when the camera is very close behind Boris and is pursuing him as it is being pursued by the viewer's eye, draw the spectator visually into the action and make that spectator feel both pursuer and pursued. The rhythms of the pursuit are accentuated by the loud gunfire, the barking dogs, and the pluckings of a stringed instrument. The pursuit continues for several minutes, and the length of time taken for this sequence of film allows the spectator to pay attention to details in the scene, to repetitions, and to variations. Three times during the pursuit, Boris either falls down or leaps forward to the ground, each time giving the impression that he has been shot. The fourth time, he clutches his heart before he falls and then lies immobile in the bushes. In spite of the previous false alarms, the spectator now believes that Boris has been killed or seriously wounded.

4 / PERCEPTION AND DECEPTION

However, the next morning he wakes up, brushes his jacket, washes his face in a brook, and continues walking. As he walks, a voice-over begins telling his story, which is interrupted by the shots of the women playing blind man's buff. Their game is a second form of flight. It ends when Boris appears in the doorway of the room in which they are playing.

A third version of flight involves Boris and Jean. Boris describes for the women his relationship with Jean and his attempt to rescue Jean from the Germans. The scene is re-created for us. Again, a hand-held camera follows them through the woods as they head for a hiding place, the way it had followed Boris in the beginning. Like Boris, Jean appears to be shot, but when Boris leaves to find a doctor, Jean seems to recover.

In a fourth flight, Jean escapes from a makeshift German prison, an escape supposedly engineered by Boris. He is also wounded during this flight but is shown being taken up some stairs, rather than to a hiding place in the woods.

A variation on the meaning of flight is Boris's amorous pursuit of a willing Maria in the woods. The last shots of the sequence are in her room, where the pace of the closeups and reverse angle shots and the laughter and heavy breathing emphasize the excitement. We also see him slapping her. The pursuit and the brutality mirror the other pursuits and imply their sexual nature.

As Boris sleeps in Maria's bed, he has his dream of pursuit. The sexual encounter and the relationship to the pursuers become even more explicit by this juxtaposition.

Another flight is Jean's escape through an underground passage that begins at the pharmacy. In the version told by the barmaid, he succeeds with help from the girl in the pharmacy. In Boris's version, the girl betrays him; in the image we see, Boris is with Jean and possibly pushes him off a ledge in the tunnel. However, the voice-over storyteller says, "At the risk of my life I went down to him."

Boris's next flight is from the ghostly, invisible Jean. He wakes up in Sylvie's bed and leaves the room backwards, with his hand held protectively before his face, as the camera pursues him. He talks disconnectedly in the direction of the camera. The rooms he enters are crowded with discarded items, and he bumps into them. Finally, in a frenzy, he bursts into a room, which turns out to be the room where the corpse of the father is laid out.

The final flight and pursuit is a recapitulation of the first images: Boris is in the woods, looking back expectantly as he is pursued by the hand-held camera. There is a sound of crashing chords and some of the other sounds of the opening images, but there is no gunfire.

Motif 2, *Seduction and Betrayal*, grows out of the variations on the theme of flight. Having established his close relationship with Jean by his first words, Boris tries very hard to usurp Jean's position in every way. He sleeps with the maid, seduces Jean's sister, and makes many overtures to Jean's wife. She evades him, but finally he tells her he is going to take her by force. Boris's seductions, successful and unsuccessful, are shown, not told.

Boris tries to appropriate Jean's reputation too. In his first story to the women, he implies that he must save Jean from despair as well as from pursuing soldiers. In a later version of the escape-from-prison story, one which he tells to Maria as Sylvie eavesdrops, he denounces Jean as a coward, traitor, and imposter. He tells yet another version of his relationship to Jean and to Jean's capture later on to Sylvie. He "admits" he has acted cowardly and enacts his own public execution by Jean and the Underground fighters. Sylvie calls him crazy.

As a variation on the stories of loyalty betrayed, the father falls from a balcony, or is possibly pushed by his servant Frantz.

The final betrayal occurs with the final seduction. Boris dramatically declares to Laura that Jean's spirit lives and has chosen to inhabit him, Boris. Laura ignores him, and he turns on Sylvie. He tells her that he has killed her brother, "an impotent, frightened man." As he caresses her, he tells her he wanted everything Jean had had, including his wife. He has taken Sylvie along the way, he says. The climactic moment of the Seduction and Betrayal motif comes when Boris is menacing Laura and Jean appears in the doorway and shoots him. As a final twist, when Boris is lying on the floor, seemingly dead, Laura bends over him tenderly, whispering one of the few words she speaks out loud in the film—"Boris."

4 / PERCEPTION AND DECEPTION

Motif 3, *Haunting*, affects the atmosphere and the tone of the film. All of the characters act like ghosts: Boris in his sudden apparitions, Jean in his ubiquitous presence, and the silent, spying women. The house is like a haunted house with its debris, its old portraits and old-fashioned furniture, and its framing doorways and winding corridors. There are many arches and oval portraits and mirrors, all suggesting a looking-glass interior, as in the book *Alice through the Looking Glass*.[10]

Boris is like a ghost in a number of ways: he claims he is known in the town, but nobody recognizes him. When he is talking to Maria in the attic, Frantz enters and talks to her but ignores Boris as though he does not see him. When he enters his room at the inn, he switches on the light, and then we see him sitting on the bed looking toward the door, as though he has been watching himself turn on the light. He treats himself like an apparition: he claims to Laura that he is just the body to contain the reincarnation of Jean; he tells Maria that he is already dead, shot as a traitor by the members of the Resistance; and finally he rises from the floor after being shot by Jean and begins his story all over again.

Jean is an apparition brought to life by the stories Boris tells about him. At the beginning, he is a memory for the townspeople. He is the link that keeps the three women at the chateau bound to each other. He is the persona that Boris tries to imitate and take over. He literally haunts and pursues Boris in the chateau after Boris has slept with Sylvie. "Why are you persecuting me?" Boris cries to the empty space. After the last story Boris tells, in which he talks about footsteps found around the buried coffin supposedly containing Jean's body, Jean appears in person.

A variation on the haunting motif is the game of blind man's buff. The women chase each other and try to touch each other. The blindfolded woman seems to be playing erotic games with ghosts, until Boris enters the room and she touches his face.

Motif 4, *Metamorphosis*, is, first of all, part of the filmmaking process. Almost all the effects of any film involve some change in the image. When shots are cut, the image seems to disappear. Abrupt cutting between images achieves effects of change or distortion. Viewing a character from different camera angles changes his appearance. Freeze shots stop the movement and life of a scene. Space and time are manipulated by the length of shots and by changes in scene.

In Boris's retelling of Jean's escape in the underground passage, the girl in the pharmacy is shown encountering the soldiers guarding the road. In a series of frozen shots, she communicates to the soldiers that Jean is escaping by a certain route. Each freeze shot is a pose. Her facial expressions are exaggerated, and her hands are raised expressively, or she bends over and whispers to a soldier, or the expression on a soldier's face is a caricature of a villainous look. The sequence is a little melodrama in which the pharmacist is enacting a betrayal of her friends. The freeze shots have betrayed her, and thus her character has been changed for us by the cinematic technique, not by the words she speaks. However, the actions are so exaggerated that the storyteller's reliability can be questioned. Either she is acting or the storyteller is lying. Both acting and lying change or metamorphose reality.

Another lengthy sequence, called by Robbe-Grillet in his notes "Maria punie," enacts a mock trial, a mock judgment, and a mock near-execution of Maria, presumably for sleeping with Boris. In his preliminary notes, Robbe-Grillet envisioned the scene this way:

> It is necessary to film this scene with many shots of which the exact use will be decided during the editing; these shots, generally very brief, will be devoted in turn either to the moment of total immobility of the three young women, or to a gesture of one or the other, a theatrical gesture of the hand, a movement of the whole body, a simple change of glance, some words (silent) articulated in closeup, etc. All this must be played with much seriousness, in spite of excessiveness, and must not make the spectator laugh (smile, barely, now and then).[11]

In its final form, the scene is an elaborate pantomime. The fragmentation of the images makes each object and action equally important; the old chandelier, Laura's foot, the candlestick with the sharp prong, and the wheel are all suggestive enough to have multiple meanings, but because of the quick cutting and the random order of the shots, the pattern of the objects becomes more important than the individual meanings they might have. They

4 / PERCEPTION AND DECEPTION

are presented to be looked at rather than to be thought about. Fragmented and out of context, they are shapes without a clearly symbolic function.

As Robbe-Grillet suggests, the solemnity of the pantomime could be funny, but the pace and randomness do not really develop the humor. The pace and randomness were deliberately designed to allow each shot to be an isolated fragment:

> I filmed a series of shots impossible to link together, so that it was the work of the editing, which was of paramount importance, to do so. I filmed five sequences of five scenes: the accusation, the speech for the defense, the entreaty, the verdict, and the execution. Then, in the interior of each scene, a series of closeups that did not present any possibility of linkage: gestures, objects, diverse details. This material demands the creation of an improbable editing, that potentially frees a very strong energy.[12]

André Gardies has suggested that Robbe-Grillet means he wants the "energy" of the shots to produce "outgrowth" or "development."[13] Since the shots cannot be linked coherently, development must be from the individual shots. Each shot has its own impact, and the whole does not equal more than the sum of its parts in meaning. The trial does not metamorphose into anything real. The execution is a mock beheading, and the women burst out laughing at the end. The laughing becomes a link to the next scene. The next shot is a closeup of the laughing barmaid. The following shot shows us the women again, still laughing. The third shot shows us the barmaid again, but she is with Boris, not with the women. Although it isn't clear that she knows about the trial game, she makes the comment, "They're all crazy, you know." We assume she is talking about the women, but the assumption is made only because of the juxtaposition of the shots.

There are several minor metamorphoses that are the result of cinematic technique. Boris leaps onto the bed as he explains to Sylvie the plan for Jean's escape from the prison, and his leap becomes Jean's leap onto some rafters in the house where he is imprisoned. In another example, Boris falls onto the ground with his hand over his heart after we see a scene of his execution by the partisans, and this fall is concluded in the next shot on the floor of the bedroom where he is telling the story to Sylvie.

The contamination shots (of the three women) in the opening sequence of the film are like foreshadowings of metamorphosis, in that they show us a scene in which there is a form of flight—dodging the blindfolded woman—and at the same time direct the audience's attention to another time, place, action by making it immediately present. The audience's attention is transported, metamorphosed, enlarged.

A final act of magic and metamorphosis occurs in the last sequence. Boris has arisen from the dead and is telling his story again. He is seen in closeup. Then he turns in profile as he talks, and then turns back again. The face we now see is that of Jean, though the voice is still that of Boris. In the last shot, as the voice continues the story, Boris is shown running in the forest.

The four motifs are closely interwoven. Each shot or sequence is created by a complex interrelationship or matrix of motifs, all of which have developed from the opening shots of the film. In the opening shots, there were flight, a false impression, and uncertainty; then the storytelling began. At intervals during the film, Boris repeats the phrase, "Let me tell you my story," by which he introduces each new development and variation on a motif. Aleatory inspiration also helped create the development of the film. Each day Robbe-Grillet used the material that had already been filmed to determine the action for that day.[14] The initial scenes were written out or outlined, but after that he did not have a prepared text or a prepared set:

> As was the practice for the last works of Robbe-Grillet, the initial scenes were written with much more precision than the following, of which the aleatory character is progressively accentuated until the ending, which is left completely open. (ibid)

The process is evolutionary. Images and scenes expand into more complex forms; sometimes there are mutations, such as the contradictory stories. The construction of the work occurs by chance and by deliberate motif-generation. As a film (and as in *L'Immortelle*), sound as well as image is a source of pattern in the film. The camera manipulates our vision by the look and movement of the images, and a sound track adds another level of response. Robbe-Grillet has used sound and image and combinations of

4 / PERCEPTION AND DECEPTION

sound and image for their own sakes, not as subordinate elements in a story, as noted by Dominique Chateau:

> All the sight and sound, carefully done and reiterated in this film, inspires the four following reflexions. First, the number of sounds used is of little importance; I have counted 44. Second, their quasi-totality is given in the first reel. Third, the majority of them have more than one occurrence. Fourth, in general, a second occurrence does not respect the audio-visual liaisons of the first. . . . [T]hese observations, are, in my opinion, full of consequences. Robbe-Grillet and Fano work on a collection of sounds well controlled and circumscribed, reunited at the beginning of the film in order to establish the form of the matrix, distributed by what follows in various combinations, but free to figure in as much of the context as possible. . . . [T]hese rules . . . are, in one sense, constraining, permitting creativity in a material universe and delimited set of themes, excluding all sorts of elements that chance or life would cause to spring up in narrative films. They are at the same time free, permitting creativity at the level of structuration, excluding the exclusive return to the narrative code.[15]

The major point of Chateau's remarks is that creativity or originality is the only purpose of the complex sound pattern. Neither "imitation" of life nor "the narrative code" (that is, the conventions of storytelling) directs the pattern of sounds of the works; there is no strictly logical meaning in the recurrence of sounds or in their relationships to the image. This "free" use of sounds is in fact delimiting: it excludes elements that would point to "imitation" as do the conventions of narrative films.

The film is an ambitious attempt to use the power of music and its forms of development to *move* (in all senses) the viewer to react to this experience. As is true for music, the audience's sensual reaction is very important and hard to define. In discussing significance in music, Susanne Langer offers a definition that may sum up the musical effect of *The Man Who Lies*:

> The assignment of meanings is a shifting, kaleidoscopic play, probably below the threshold of consciousness, certainly outside the place of discursive thinking. The imagination that responds to music is personal and associative and logical, tinged with affect, tinged with bodily rhythm, tinged with dream, but *concerned* with a wealth of formulations for its wealth of wordless knowledge.[16]

But since the film is verbal as well as aural, some of the knowledge intended is not entirely wordless, nor are the formulations of knowledge kept entirely personal. The characters have individual shapes, and the places and events are real or close to a past reality: the Carpathians and the last war. Parody and comic irony pervade the narrative. The protean narrator who lies so ingratiatingly and who mocks himself and the other characters constantly is the audience's spiritual guide through the events. In the collection of essays *Robbe-Grillet and the Fantastic*, several essays identify Robbe-Grillet himself as the protean narrator:

Thomas Spear: "[H]e is a writer who toys with a serious personal and polemical engagement presented in his *romanesques* texts yet this textual identity slides, elusively and ultimately, into the realm of fabrication."[17]

Ralph Yarrow: "PROPOSITION: Robbe-Grillet is discoverable only in the play of his work. When he is most himself, he plays most. Boris, Robin, JR. etc. Jean ou Djinn" (35).

The most protean of narrators structures the novel *Djinn* (1981), which uses new narrators for succeeding chapters, and the reader must watch the pronouns or the description to detect the gender or whether there is a first- or third-person narration in each chapter. Detection is the subject of the novel, and detection is the job of the reader. Whether it is "us"—possibly government investigators—in the prologue, or the first "I" (a young man named Boris), the teller of events changes. The "us" has discovered a typewritten manuscript written in the first person, which becomes the third person when an omniscient narrator in chapter 6 now is describing a man named Simon, who, in the middle of the chapter, turns into an "I" Simon; the "I" Simon continues to narrate through part of chapter 7, and he then becomes again a Simon being described by an omniscient narrator until the end of that chapter. In chapter 8, the narrator is female and is an "I" narrator, who has met by chance "a guy my age named Simon Lecoeur, who was known as Boris, I never knew why."[18]

4 / PERCEPTION AND DECEPTION

An epilogue concludes the novel with a return to the mysterious investigators, who begin the chapter with the comment, "So stops Simon Lecoeur's story," having decided that the female narrator was simply a role assumed by Simon, alias Boris. They had also decided in the prologue that "the ratio of probability of the reported events is almost always too low, in relation to the laws of traditional realism" (10).

Shifting points of view—if the changing of names and genders can be called points of view—accompany a cyclic telling of a story, with the mysterious figure of Djinn (an American woman) at the center. Djinn is at times a real person, or a recording of a voice, or a mannequin. Djinn is androgynous; Djinn is a revolutionary or a figurehead for a group of terrorists or a joke that Boris is playing on the investigators.

The tenses of the chapters change—from present, to past, to future—thereby playing with fictional time, without the usual device of flashback or flashforward. Or perhaps, as the "investigators" say, Simon's discovered narrative is like an exercise in a language text, with tenses being illustrated.

A child named Marie is part of one of the recycled stories that Simon/Boris tells, and Marie is described at various times as a "champion liar"; she makes up stories about the waiter in the pizza restaurant, and she criticizes Simon/Boris for the tense he uses in a story he is telling her and for his general incompetency as a writer: "The ending is idiotic. . . . You had a few good ideas, but you did not know how to exploit them intelligently" (48). Simon's comment about her is that "Marie, like all children and poets, enjoys playing with sense and nonsense" (49).

Memory is another playful device causing reassemblages of the story. A child named Jean (Marie's brother) has an "afflicted" memory that predicts future events and brings them to real life; Simon also comments that "we believe in things that are quite false; it is enough that some fragment of memory, come from elsewhere, enters into some coherent pattern open to it, or else that we unconsciously fuse two disparate halves, or still that we reverse the order of the elements in some causal system, to fashion in our minds chimerical objects, having for us all the appearances of reality" (86).

Finally, there is the question of blindness and free will. The dominant narrator, Simon/Boris, is fascinated by Djinn, the American woman or image of a woman, who directs him in the mysterious adventure that recurs through the book, finally requiring him to assume a disguise as a blind man, wearing dark glasses and carrying a cane. In this state, he comments that a blind person can no longer do anything secretly. After he listens to Djinn lecturing on "alienation by the machine, which has brought forth capitalism and Soviet bureaucracy," he is disturbed: "They want to raise our consciousness, but they start out by preventing us from seeing" (70). Simon's final comment on his blindness is ironic, reflective of Robbe-Grillet's often expressed attitude about ideology and belief systems: "[T]his darkness to which I am condemning myself, and which I doubtlessly enjoy, seems to fit perfectly the mental uncertainty in which I have been struggling since waking up. My self-imposed blindness would be some sort of metaphor for it, or its objective correlative, or a redundancy" (89).

Robbe-Grillet is not lying about the deception that is part of novelistic practice. The reader follows clues laid out for him/her by the author/narrator and obeys that guided path, only occasionally peeking from behind self-imposed dark glasses to question the imagined situation and landscape. In fact, since peeking creates disillusionment, it is better for the purposes of responding to art to allow the mental uncertainty of the real world to be kept at bay. Robbe-Grillet is high-handed; he insists that we look twice, three times, four times at the novel's or film's progress and connections; no story is the only story, no set of connections is the definitive set of connections. The appearances of reality are constantly shifting—mannequins look real and real dead women are found lying in blood that is not real.

Where is the author? For Roland Barthes, "the modern scriptor is born simultaneously with the text, is in no way equipped with a being preceding or exceeding the writing."[19] On the other hand, Robbe-Grillet has the final word on the constant presence and overpowering influence of the author: "I have never spoken of anything but myself. From within, and so it has hardly been noticed. Fortunately."[20]

4 / PERCEPTION AND DECEPTION

The author, the Robbe-Grillet author, does not seek attention or analysis or influence as an author. His comic irony may betray his position, but his permissive acceptance of any kind of audience response encourages rejection of his authorial authority.

Narrator and narrative have been exposed and questioned in *The Man Who Lies* and *Djinn*, but not the art of narration. Characters in his works seem compelled to tell stories—unbelievable, fantastic, untrue, usually—but the stories use events, carefully described. His sixth novel, *Topologie d'une cité fantôme* (*Topology of a Phantom City*) tells complicated, seemingly interwoven stories and is relentlessly descriptive, generative, and fantastic. Narrators of all sorts tell the stories but remain aloof from the events, defying the readers to make connections.

5
Vision, Visualization, and Interpenetration

The novel *Topology of a Phantom City* is an assemblage[1] or collage of previously written material. The materials, all of them written in collaboration with visual artists (and one of them for a whiskey advertisement), have been put together by Robbe-Grillet in such a manner that they seem to be developing images and motifs and constructing a single story, or at least interrelated stories. Certain images and motifs do keep recurring, partly because the previously written work has been broken up: part of the Robert Rauschenberg material appears in the *Incipit*; part in the first subsection, *Fifth Space;* and the rest in subsections 3 and 4, *Fifth Space;* part of the Paul Delvaux material is in *First Space* and the rest in *Third Space;* part of the David Hamilton material constitutes *Second Space* and the rest of David Hamilton's work constitutes subsection 1 and subsection 2 of *Fourth Space*. Subsection 5 of *Fifth Space* is the opening section or first chapter of a collaborative work with René Magritte. And all of the images and motifs are part of Robbe-Grillet's visual and literary language and appear in many of his works.

Like the collage elements in synthetic cubism, or the constructions and assemblages of post-abstract expressionist American artists of the 1950s and 1960s, or the paintings and the writings of many surrealists, *Topology of a Phantom City* uses chance, an unpredictable sense of order, and unpredictable results. Twentieth-century visual art has been in the vanguard of challenging audience reactions and demanding new ways of seeing. As Wallace Fowlie says in discussing surrealism,

5 / VISION, VISUALIZATION

> [C]hance coalitions which may take place in free imaginative states of mind are more valuable in the making of art than the logical juxtapositions we impose upon words and sounds and colors in our trained, consciously focused states of mind.[2]

In *Topology of a Phantom City*, words and sequences of action and description are placed in unexpected juxtapositions and are blended by the process of reading.

Robbe-Grillet has surrealist attachments: his choices of Paul Delvaux and Rene Magritte as collaborators, his use of dream-like images and sexual motifs. But, as is usual in Robbe-Grillet's ideological or aesthetic attachments, his concerns are not surrealist concerns. He is not dedicated to changing man's perception of the *world*, but of *art*; he is not trying to break down the barriers between people and to rediscover love and brotherhood, as André Breton demanded. He does not declare great confidence in man's potential, as Ferdinand Alquié has stated:

> [The surrealists'] works tend ... to enlarge the human domain, to liberate unknown and unconscious forces that are in man, to render to man and man alone all that belongs to him, that is to say all that he can think and dream and conceive.[3]

What Robbe-Grillet does want can only be discovered by examining this work, part by part, movement by movement. Perhaps to parody conventional resumes written for book covers, there is a *prière d'inserer* (an inserted, extraneous?, entreaty) on the cover of the French edition that seems to be a summary:

> A lost city that had been shielded on the same territory for several successive civilizations—repetitive or contradictory—each one depositing its strata (its particular topography, its history marked out by natural cataclysms or by massacres, its sacred texts, its panoply of utensils and of signs) gives rise here to a sort of cross-section where different systems of tracts reveal the proper space of each age. But the fragments overlap, interpenetrate, mutually destroy each other. . . . Theaters, prisons, harems, temples and lupanars appear nevertheless to the archeologist, who advances step by step into this maze moving toward sudden transformations, to contain (to hide, or very much to the contrary, more often, to put forward) the same secret crime: the

complicated and ceremonial murder of a barely nubile prostitute, of which the memory—or the ritual reproduction—leaves suspect stains on the steps of the investigator. Thus the child who returns already recognizes these still fresh impressions—the sexual fantasies which the nurturing society has outlined for him in his text books, his art books, or history books, or of religion, all of which tell him in their own deceitful manner, tirelessly, about the same desire.

The author, never explicitly presented as author, has taken the role of archeologist-investigator. As the resume suggests, the archeological ages are called "Spaces" and constitute the divisions of the book. Within each Space there are scenes of action and partially identified characters, who reappear in other Spaces because of the way Robbe-Grillet carved up the work he had already previously produced.

The description of each Space is in the present tense and is told as if the observer were in the process of seeing the actual places and events. Each Space is named: *First Space*, "Construction of a ruined temple to the goddess Vanadis"; *Second Space*, "Ascending rehearsals for a motionless dwelling"; *Third Space*, "Construction of a ruined temple (continued and concluded)"; *Fourth Space*, "Reveries of young girls confined between window and looking-glass"; *Fifth Space*, "The criminal already on my trail." An *Incipit* and a *Coda* complete the divisions of the book.

All of these parts of the novel, except the *Coda*, were written for earlier works in which Robbe-Grillet collaborated with several artists: Robert Rauschenberg, the American painter; Paul Delvaux, the Belgian painter; David Hamilton, the English photographer; and René Magritte, the French painter. Bruce Morrissette, in his study *Intertextual Assemblage in Robbe-Grillet*, summarizes these collaborations in a special appendix.[4] The following is a paraphrase of his summary:

1. *Incipit* is also the opening section of Robbe-Grillet's collaborative work with the lithographs of Robert Rauschenberg, entitled *Traces suspectes en surface*, published after 1979.

2. *First Space* is the first seven subtitled texts, each accompanied by an original etching by Paul Delvaux, from the Delvaux-Robbe-Grillet

5 / VISION, VISUALIZATION

volume entitled *Construction d'un temple en ruines à la Déese Vanade* (Construction of a temple in ruins to the Goddess Vanadis), 1975.

3. *Second Space* was first published as "La Demeure immobile de David Hamilton" in the periodical *Zoom* (5 [December 1970]). In the novel, it is called "Ascending rehearsals for a motionless dwelling."

4. *Third Space* is the remaining three subtitled sections of the collaborative work with Paul Delvaux. In the novel, it is called "Construction of a ruined temple (continued and concluded)."

5. *Fourth Space* has several parts. Subsection 1, entitled here "Affected vagrancy meanwhile," consists of ten brief titled texts related to photographs by David Hamilton, originally published as *Rêves des jeunes filles* (Dreams of young girls), 1971. Subsection 2, entitled in the novel "Second initiatory cycle," contains twelve brief, titled texts related to other photographs by Hamilton, published as *Les Demoiselles d'Hamilton* (*Sisters*), 1972.

6. *Fifth Space* is divided into five subsections. The first subsection, entitled here "Return erased," forms part of the collaborative work with Rauschenberg *Traces suspectes en surface*; the second subsection, entitled here "Ritual ceremony," was originally commissioned by the Japanese liquor company Suntory and appeared widely in Japanese newspapers sometime prior to 1975. Subsections 3 and 4, entitled here "Landscape with cry" and "The excavations in retrospect," are the final parts of the Rauschenberg collaboration *Traces suspectes en surface*. Subsection 5, entitled here "A double-backed altar," forms the opening section, or first chapter, of the Robbe-Grillet–Magritte work entitled *La Belle Captive*, 1975.

As we see, most of the novel had a previous existence in other contexts. In this new context, and because of their new connections with each other, they change in purpose and suggestiveness, but their previous existence and their new existence are still connected. In the surrealist sense, Robbe-Grillet is "[reconciling] two distinct realities on a new and unexpected plane," according to Lucy Lippard.[5] As usual, Robbe-Grillet is elaborating on that concept, using realities originally conceived in several minds, which had been influenced in each creation by collaboration with his mind. Visual reality and verbal reality had originally been related, or made harmonious, "reconciled," as they were experienced. The verbal descriptions and the visual imagery had connections with each other both originally and in their new existence in this book. The reader either rejects the new juxtapositions or accepts them and tries to create some order from this confusion of elements.

One way to create order in the reading experience, suggested by the arrangement of the whole structure, is to follow a musical model. The *Incipit* is the introduction, motifs make up the body of the material, and the *Coda* is the conclusion. In music, the terms *incipit*, *motif*, and *coda* serve very definite functions. Incipit (Latin: it begins) constitutes the first words of a Gregorian chant, of the liturgical text, sung by the cantor before the chorus picks up the text at a specifically marked place.[6] The motif, or motive, is

> the briefest intelligible and self-contained fragment of a musical theme or subject. The motives are the very bricks or the germinating cells of the musical composition. It is through their highly developed use (repetition in the same or in other parts; transposition into other pitches; rhythmical modifications; contrapuntal combination with other motives) that Bach ... has bestowed upon his work a unique quality of logical coherence and well-motivated organization." (462)

Coda (Italian: tail) is "a section of a composition which is added to the form proper as a conclusion" (159).

It is evident that these terms of musical structure bear a startling resemblance to the structure of *Topology of a Phantom City*. Instead of clock time, the novel uses musical motives (motifs) and phrases that link paragraphs, shift the movement of the action, and finally link the numbered Spaces. The Spaces are related to the concept of topography, suggested by the word *topology*, as defined in one of its meanings: "Topographical study of a particular place; specif., the history of a region as indicated by its topography."[7]

In mathematics, topology is the doctrine of those properties of a figure unaffected by any deformation, without tearing or joining (ibid.). According to Bruce Morrissette, the mathematical process of topology is a way of revealing everything about a geometric figure, and by metaphoric extension, about any material entity.

5 / VISION, VISUALIZATION 107

[The process of topology reveals surfaces, volumes, boundaries, contiguities, holes, and above all the notions of *inside* and *outside*, with the attendant ideas of insertion, penetration, containment, emergence, and the like.

Topographically, Robbe-Grillet is describing the surface details of the place (the Phantom City) and the relationship of the component parts. Using the mathematical-metaphoric process, he then retains the ritual murder as the central "property" that remains unchanged no matter what else changes, and he traces it in various times and places and describes it from many perspectives—as myth, as pictorial depiction, as theatrical performance.

All of this has been very inventively done after the initial creation of the images and forms, all of which, after all, originally were created in Robbe-Grillet's mind. Shifting narrators (shifting Robbe-Grillets?) conduct the description as investigation of the place and its parts. No single consciousness seems to be in control, but all of them are in the domain of the dream state. The universe of the dream state involves a free exchange of mental imagery among several characters, who enter the scenes, change forms, combine with each other, and are sometimes revealed as the creators, particularly the creators of art, all working on a continuing creation.

In the dream state, condensation and displacement produce images that are the distortion of the events of real life. Real life is the source but it is manipulated inventively in the dream state; the dream state becomes another reality, in which, as Robbe-Grillet noted in his essay on Joë Bousquet, "our imagination is the organizing force of our life, of our world."[8] Through imagination, which works as we sleep, the materials of the real world can be moved, blended, reshaped, and refreshed. Motifs, particularly from artworks, also structure this creation, as they are introduced as words, objects, events, and places. They, the motifs, have been generated, and they become transformed, metamorphosed.

How the Structure Is Generated

The phrase "Before I fall asleep," which occurs six times in the three pages of the *Incipit*, initiates and then reiterates the dream state of the narrator. The repetition of the phrase is, as in musical repetition, a motif. It helps to prepare the reader for the visions of the dream, as they are described in the *Incipit* and as they will be presented in the rest of the work. The narrator, using the first-person form, has several visions that he or she describes.

The dominant vision is of a ruined city. Phrases describing the destruction keep recurring. The dream becomes a memory, or an attempt to create a memory. It is as though the unconscious were trying to dig deep into its primitive past to discover the actual look of that place. As the dream and memory seem to fuse (signaled humorously by "the iridescent mist through which flocks of sheep pass in endless procession"[9]), the "I" narrator enters the ruined city, inscribes the word "Construction" on a wall, and calls the inscription an "illusionist" or trompe-l'oeil painting. (13) As trompe-l'oeil, the inscription suggests that all that follows is an illusion of reality, a false appearance of reality.

First Space, part 1, "In the generative cell," is literally a prison cell. It is described in detail as containing a series of rectangular tableaux, the number of tableaux having some significance according to the calculations of the "I" narrator (20). Everything—including the shape of the tarot card, the shape of the table, and the shape of the sheet of paper on which are inscribed by hand "the rules of the game"—is included in the calculation of the number of rectangular objects.

A number of games are being played in the cell: a card game, a murder game, a voyeur game, and an artist-model game. Connections are made among groups and among games by identical postures or by similar figure groupings. In the artist-model group, the artist's posture, orientation, and wooden chair are "exactly like those of the card player in the foreground who is looking at the patch of sunlight on the wall" (18). In the meantime, the painter is looking at some onlookers, who are "dressed and arranged in the same way" (18) and who are looking at another group, whose members seem to be arranged to perform an operation (19).

5 / VISION, VISUALIZATION

All of these tableaux, so precisely described, are in fact in the head of the narrator, who reminds us of this in two ways: he is not sure of the meaning of some little lines drawn on the wall, and he corrects himself about the image of the chairs: "I was wrong when I spoke above of chairs of painted wood" (19).

Part 2, "Outside, the lengthened shadow," brings events of the outside into the cell. Two scenes, in sharp contrast to each other, are juxtaposed. The first scene describes a wounded, naked girl running down a road from a temple on the top of a hill. Yet as soon as the narrator describes the temple, he dismisses his description as an improbable architectural model, again emphasizing the fact that the scene is being re-created in his mind. He switches instead to a scene in a partially destroyed city, which then metamorphoses into the same site, now cleared of rubble for tourists, in which young women wearing long dresses, corsets, and boots are walking. Three time periods have been compressed into one Space and three paragraphs. All of the described scenes are occurring, we are reminded (23–24), outside the walls of the prison (containing the generative cell), a place that seems to be part of the tourist route.

A small pebble lying on the ground under the windows of the prison connects the scenes above to the next part, part 3, "Pebble and stylet." As the young ladies are looking at the prison, inside another metamorphosis has occurred. The painter is in fact an engraver, who is using a "slender steel stylet" (27) on a sheet of polished copper and is making a very accurate representation of the hand of the model. One flaw is pointed out: when the engraving is printed, the image will be reversed, and "the final image performs with its right hand the gesture that the live model is executing with her left" (27).

Another transformation in the image occurs: the chairs have changed. Another rectangular area is noticed: a trapdoor. And again the "I" interferes, describing himself as "the narrator," whose head obscures a viewing of what is going on, as though the lens of his mind were focusing on a limited area and his projected self were part of that area. Then yet another transformation occurs: the painting that has become an engraving now becomes a drawing, and it depicts the naked and wounded girl who was mentioned at the beginning of the last part. The final paragraph of this part summarizes quickly a number of actions occurring one after another. The paragraph concludes with a cry from under the trapdoor.

The description in the next two parts—4, "The inscription," and 5, "The ship of sacrifice"—re-creates a mythological event. The existence of an ancient city, a destruction by a volcano, and the survival of a group of prisoners in the women's prison are part of the story being told to the convalescent girl prisoner who is in the room under the trapdoor. The convalescent dreams another story—that of the hermaphrodite god of pleasure, Vanadis, who impregnated the women of the ancient city, all of whom then bore females "until a periodic irruption of enemy soldiers into the vanquished city" (34).

A number of descriptions blend into each other: "his ambiguous genitals also form a kind of butterfly in the hollow of his thighs" (35) becomes "white or black butterflies flit in search of absent flowers" on the sea (35). And on the sea is a vessel with a superstructure like the temple on the hill in part 3. The warriors on the ship are described, as is a banner at the top of the mast that has a letter G. In the next paragraph, the letter on the banner engenders a series of words using *v*s, *d*s, and *g*s, in the form of a poem. The poem tells the story of the rape of the virgin and the birth of David, the demigod, male counterpart of Vanadis. His mother, the raped young girl, is revealed as the "victim . . . fleeing from the temple and running toward the absent portion of the drawing" (38). The whole story is thus transformed into pictorial form, not only by the reference to the drawing but also by a casual reference to "the next engraving" in which the injured girl is "climbing the rocky strip back onto the quiet quay and its polished flagstones" (39).

Part 4 is "Intermission," and the whole story is put into the perspective of a theatrical performance. The audience relaxes by promenading on the boulevard, and a number of scenes parody some of the previously recited events: several young girls are bathing, and one of them is caught by a group of architectural students; a man and a woman watching a Sunday painter stand in the same pose as the onlookers in "the generative cell"; two digni-

5 / VISION, VISUALIZATION

fied ladies are talking about a birth by Caesarean section. A young matron is introduced, with her two children named Deana and David, and they pause to examine the sign for the theatrical performance "The Birth of David." Finally, in the last part of *First Space* (part 7), "Hypothetical birth of David G.," we are back in the theater. One of the tableaux being presented involves a young girl photographer, who is looking in her viewfinder at a scene of two young girls helping each other bathe. A second tableau is presented in which a sleeping girl is being watched by two other girls, and the third tableau is of four people playing cards. A card in the middle of the table is being pointed to and focussed on:

> a naïvely drawn picture of a tall, solidly built tower flaring at its base in a gigantic blaze as if the very stone were on fire, while right at the top, on the narrow circular balcony, a young woman holding her two children by the hand is anxiously scanning the horizon of the sea, apparently still looking to it for assistance at this eleventh hour. (49)

The mother and children who were looking at the theatrical announcement have been made part of the performance by their representation on the card. In the next paragraph, they have come alive, but they are on the top of the tower. The mother is describing the town, which is spread out below. While he is looking down, the boy drops a pebble wrapped in a sheet of paper from a school exercise book—like the paper on which were written the rules of the game in the girls' prison and like the paper the architectural students were crumbling and throwing into the pond as they watched the bathing girls.

The mother and the children begin to descend the tower by means of a spiral staircase. From small windows along the way, they see the "same scenes all over again, gone through in the reverse order this time and at a much quicker pace" (51). On their way, they see the theater and the three thousand spectators. They end their descent in the initial cell, which leads them through the trapdoor into the "execution cell," and the last word they hear is "the Caesarean." The last image the boy sees is a "reddish brown fresco, faded and eroded with the years, that is painted on the back wall" (52).

The last paragraph of the last part of *First Space* describes a later time—"thirty years later"—when the boy is grown and is having dreams of climbing staircases with "the same halts, bifurcations, sudden breaks and resumptions" (53). The dreams are a recreation of his journey and in fact of the movement of the novel. Next, he is described as watching a performance of a work whose rehearsals he has often watched. He notes a discrepancy that bothers him: the changed letter on the streamer of "the ship of sacrifice" (53). The letter is now *H*, we later find out.

> He is in a hurry to rediscover, outside, the lengthened shadow. But he has to wait until everything is motionless again, the cycle as a whole having been closed by a specious, non-recurring, descending movement in the generative cell. (53)

Second Space, "Ascending rehearsals for a motionless dwelling," is an extended description of David H.'s ascent up the staircase, through the corridors, and in and out of the rooms of an old house, each area revealing to his dreams or fantasies or immediate sight young girls in states of undress. The last young girl herself has a dream. She dreams of a tableau involving several young girls, one of whom she resembles. In the next paragraph, David H. snaps his shutter and records a last image on film.

Third Space, "Construction of a ruined temple (continued and concluded)," consists of three parts: "Focus," "Dramatic turn of events," and "Provisional model of the project." An "I" narrator, who is obliquely identified with David H., is now recapitulating in his mind the events of a week. These events involve three murders of young girls, in three very different places. One murder is in the deserted house, the second in the auditorium in which the play is being presented, and the third in an archeological dig.

The events have taken place at the same time plans are proceeding for a "vast pleasure complex" in the area damaged by an explosion. This area is already the place in which "barbaric rites revived from an antiquity so remote as to be legendary" (69) are rumored to be performed.

The two opening parts of this Space are joined by the descriptions in their last paragraphs. In both descriptions, the "I" narrator slips away from other people and walks alone. In part 1, "Focus,"

5 / VISION, VISUALIZATION

he comes to "the dark river, the water flowing soundlessly, the imperceptible hisses, the smell of night, sleep" (73); in part 2, "Dramatic turn of events," he experiences "the mild, humid, night air, the smell of low tide, the dark river. By the sloping stone wall where the ripples make a sound like a dog lapping, near a flight of mooring steps, a number of white sheets are floating in a swell" (78). The second description adds more sensual imagery to the first description, thus changing the effect of the description instead of simply repeating it. This is one method—repetition with expansion of details—by which change and movement in the action of the book occur.

In part 3, "Provisional model of the project," a team of criminal investigators establishes the site for a possible fourth murder, on the map "the fourth vertex of a perfect square" (81). As the description of the site is made, the "I" narrator takes over the narration. The *Third Space* concludes with a description that seems to implicate the narrator in what he calls the "sacrifices":

> But the most hazardous measures of all will without a doubt be the construction of the Holy of Holies (in the underground part), which has to include a stake for the burnt offerings. At all events there is no question at this stage of re-opening the debate regarding the choice of the ruined building for installing the sanctuary. (86)

The *Fourth Space*, "Reveries of young girls confined between window and looking-glass," consists of fragments of thought and impressions and stories, as though told by young girls. Intertextual references to Robbe-Grillet's other works are incorporated into the recorded thoughts: the Blue Villa of Shanghai, from *The House of Assignation* (1965); the novel that takes place in Africa, described in *Jealousy* (1957); the bicycle of the voyeur, from *The Voyeur* (1955); the cruel sultans referred to in the film *The Immortal One* (1963); recurring images of the sea, from *Progressive Slippages of Pleasure* (1974); and the mirrors and corridors used in almost all the works. *Fifth Space*, "Return erased," begins at the river, where part 2 of *Third Space* concluded. A description of "return" is put in the form of memory, and the memory gradually turns into a dream. The gradual transformation is accomplished by repetition and "contamination" phrases: a sentence of description, which does not logically follow from the sentences that preceded it, is included in the whole passage. The process is repeated several times until a final paragraph concentrates on the suggestion that the narrator has been dreaming or is trying to start his narration over again:

> Now in the keener air where breathing is less oppressive, now in the warm drizzle that resumed at intervals, I walked at a steady pace through the deserted city. Yet I must have gone to bed very late; and I slept for a long time, as always. (107)
>
> What with all the detours, precautions, and feints I must have spent hours getting home. I went to bed very late and slept for a long time, as always. (108)
>
> I subsequently continue on my way through the dead city. Having gone to bed at an advanced hour of the night, I must then have slept for a very long time, as always. (109)
>
> [A]s I return to my room along the avenue planted with ageless chestnut trees, my mind a blank, as always. (109)
>
> And now here is the text: I wake up, this must have been in winter, yet I slept with the casement wide open. It is morning, it is evening. I no longer know, and the uncertain light coming in from outside does nothing to clear up the point. . . . I must have slept for a long time, probably, an indeterminate period, a blank. I remember nothing, as usual. (109–10)

In the first passage, the description shifts abruptly from walking to sleeping: is the narrator dreaming that he is walking? The second passage implies that the narrator is avoiding someone, which may fit into the action of the first passage. The third passage may be filling in the gap in the action of the first passage. The fourth passage seems to be defining a constant mental state, as indicated by "as always." In the fifth passage, the word "text" changes everything that preceded it into pretexts of a writer; this is my description, he seems to be saying. If it is accepted without logical analysis, the contamination process becomes the thought process of an artist, in whose mind images take form, arouse other

5 / VISION, VISUALIZATION 115

images, make illogical connections, and finally induce an emotional condition.

Earlier in *Topology*, in *First Space*, there were a number of passages of description in which the narrator seemed to be groping for precision in imagery. As above, the restless mind of the creator was being simulated. The language of the earlier version of mental groping was more direct:

> The immediate impression conveyed by the decor suggests that one is here in a prison. (16)

> [T]he victim (or the recalcitrant schoolgirl, or the condemned woman, or the raving lunatic, or the malingerer, or the subject of the experiment, etc.) is lying on her back. (18)

> Something more important has just come back to me; I was wrong when I spoke above of chairs of painted wood. (19)

> According to my calculations and bearing in mind the card, the tableau moving toward its conclusion, and the two wooden tables, there ought to be another rectangle in the room. (20)

> No, this architectural model is really too improbable, so is the ruined column, the remains of which would be defying the elementary laws of gravity. What there is outside is simply a lot of streets. (22)

> Remember at this point to mention the broken bar holding the attention of one group in the foreground. Point out, right at the front, a pebble the size of a fist. (24)

> But while all these details have been changing, another transformation has taken place. (27)

> [T]he precise meaning of the gestures and objects located in it is not clearly discernible, apparently because of the narrator's head coming right in front, its thick, curly hair obscuring the view. (28)

The general impression of the comments is that the scene exists, and the narrator is "seeing" it again, or conjuring it up visually in his memory. The creator is being depicted as an inspired photographer and reporter who has a special inner lens for seeing obscure events and past events. Robbe-Grillet evidently could not resist injecting a note of absurdity, as the narrator's head gets in the way of his vision.

First Space (from which the preceding descriptions were taken) comprises the first seven subtitled texts from the Paul Delvaux-Alain Robbe-Grillet book published in 1975, and *Fifth Space* (from which the walking-sleeping descriptions were taken) is part of a collaborative work with Robert Rauschenberg. Both texts were written to accompany artworks: Delvaux's etchings and Rauschenberg's lithographs. Both texts incorporate Robbe-Grillet's suggestions to the artists about how he envisioned scenes and events. In fact, when he was planning his work with Delvaux, Robbe-Grillet had already thought about the collaboration as a "dialogue":

> The more I think about it, the more I am persuaded that to obtain this interpenetration of a text and visual image ... the most amusing formula would be a dialogue. I write the first text, Delvaux replies with an engraving, which restarts my own themes and transforms them.[10]

The compositions of forms described in *First Space* are different from the actions of characters described in *Fifth Space*. This may be a reflection of a change in Robbe-Grillet's inner visions from 1975 to 1979, or it may be a reflection of the different artistic styles of his collaborators. Nevertheless, *First Space* and *Fifth Space* harmonize; they round out the construction of *Topology*. They also play with a recurring problem-motif in Robbe-Grillet's work: how to animate the visual frozen moment of an artwork by a description in a verbal work (which is in constant structural movement) and, while achieving this effect, to freeze the action of the literary work so that it simulates the suspended mood of a visual work. Many motifs in Robbe-Grillet's work become evident in the imagery of the last *Space*, motifs that have been used in the other *Spaces*, although they were all written in different years for widely different purposes. Some examples:

> Descriptions of young girls lying on divans reflect the descriptions of young girls in *Second Space* and *Fourth Space*.[11]

The letters H and G as well as the image of the young mother in *Fifth Space* (131) have previously been used in *First Space*.

The story of the ship described in *First Space* seems to be referred to in the following sentence in *Fifth Space*, "There is no point in going over the story of the ship again . . . which has already been related at ample length." (132)

On page 138 of *Fifth Space* is a sentence that seems to refer to the prison described in *First Space:* "[N]or do I stop at the chestnut-lined avenue bordering the prison, already described."

Sometimes the motifs are called "clues," and the word "clue" implies that the reader is expected to detect the images and not merely pass them by.

Part 5 of *Fifth Space* is the text of the collaborative book written by Alain Robbe-Grillet, with paintings by René Magritte, supplied by his wife, since his work had been produced many years before and he was dead. In *Topology*, only Robbe-Grillet's words are used, without the paintings; the text must carry the whole burden of meaning and structure. The relationship between word and image (their "interpenetration," as Robbe-Grillet called it) is another form of Robbe-Grillet's experiments with generators, using the challenge of static artworks to animate a narrative.

Word and Image:
The Relationship between Text and Paintings in *La Belle Captive* and the Conclusion of *Fifth Space*

The last part of *Fifth Space*, called "A double-backed altar," is the first chapter of *La Belle Captive*.[12] Along with Robbe-Grillet's text, there are nineteen of René Magritte's paintings, which are not arranged chronologically. This is the order of their use:

1. Le Chateau des Pyrénnées, 1959
2. Portrait de Femme, 1961
3. Le Monde Invisible, 1953/54
4. L'Assassin Menacé, 1926

5. Les Fleurs du Mal, 1946
6. Les Complices du Magicien, 1927
7. Le Tombeau des Lutteurs, 1960
8. La Traversée Difficile, 1926
9. La Mémoire, 1948
10. Le Domaine d'Arnheim, 1962
11. Le Sourire du Diable, 1966
12. Le Soupçon Mysterieux, 1928
13. L'Idole, 1965
14. L'Echelle du Feu, 1939
15. L'Echelle du Feu, 1933
16. Les Fanatiques, 1945
17. Le Noctambule, 1927
18. La Boîte de Pandore, 1951
19. L'Eloge de la Dialectique, 1937

The text consists of twenty-five paragraphs, each paragraph describing a scene or telling a story. The following is a summary of the paragraphs:

Para. 1: description of a falling stone, an aerolith, like a giant egg

Para. 2: description of the sea and sand

Para. 3: description of a flesh-colored rose hanging upside-down in a window and of a girl's cry

Para. 4: description of a hotel with rooms lining a long corridor with cracked walls

Para. 5: description of an interior containing a murdered dressmaker's dummy, the lines of the floor creating a perspective that continues out to the railing on the balcony outside and then beyond

Para. 6: description of a phonograph in the foreground of a room; comment—the stabbed model's body was found on the beach

Para. 7: description of a man in a room, leaning on a wooden chair, as outside in the corridor two plainclothes policemen are waiting

5 / VISION, VISUALIZATION 119

Para. 8: description of three men listening to a cry from the phonograph, as a female figure holding a rose stands in the doorway of the balcony

Para. 9: comment—the figures are Lady H-G and her children, the fraternal twins David and Vanessa; David's feelings for Vanessa are incestuous

Para. 10: description of the objects held by the policemen, especially some fish netting and a large skittle pin; recapitulation of other objects described or suggested—the falling stone, a glass of wine, the flesh-colored rose

Para. 11: reference to the phrase "the difficult crossing" and speculation about a rape

Para. 12: description of hotel, especially of men in black suits behind the railing outside an open window; description of three white eggs in a glass bowl on the window ledge

Para. 13: description of eggs as booby traps; description of a doctor who is making secret signs with his hands

Para. 14: description of scene with doctor and "I" narrator; narrator surprised as he attempts to escape through door

Para. 15: description of "I" narrator looking at the palm of his hand; description of door and key, which is hot to the touch

Para. 16: description of "I" entering a dark theater, in which the opera *The Idol* is being performed

Para. 17: description of a scene with the narrator and a blonde who is sitting next to him in the theater; narrator murmuring plot to blonde: the birth of the Phoenix from a fiery exploding egg and its flight over the cliffs

Para. 18: description of bird landing on a shoe in the rocks; the shoe, then everything else, catching fire; Vanessa appearing: she must swallow the bird that laid the egg

Para. 19: description of scene in which blonde get sick and "I" carries her to a room with a table covered by red material; doctor appearing, ready to give an injection

Para. 20: description of "I" narrator becoming a female, shedding her clothes and throwing them out the window, then walking down a street with dilapidated buildings

Para. 21: description of "I" observing a shop that sells First Communion dresses and wedding dresses

Para. 22: description of window of shop, then of "I" walking across the square to a refreshment stand, which has a red-stained tablecloth

Para. 23: description of "I" walking over the old bridge that crosses the river and meeting a young, female flower seller, who offers "I" a rose; behind is the sound of a large stone dropping from a great height into the river

Para. 24: description of "I" descending the steps to the water's edge, arriving at a place with metal structures, old buildings, wooden huts, and a huge excavation with machines that have huge searching headlights

Para. 25: description of "I" in front of his window, with a large mirror visible behind the table, reflecting the house opposite as if the outside of the room were the interior, as he reconstructs the plan of the fanatic temple

The relationships between the parts of the work, the paintings and the paragraphs, from paragraph to painting or from several paragraphs to several paintings, is constantly suggestive but never stable. The paragraphs describe objects in the paintings, and sometimes the descriptions become stories. Several stories are going on at the same time.

Paragraphs 1 through 10 seem to be setting scenes by describing people and things and places. These descriptions—the sea, a falling rock, a flesh-colored rose, a corridor with long rows of rooms, a dressmaker's dummy and a room, a phonograph, plain-clothes policemen in black suits, a fishnet, and a skittle pin—are all based on images that are in paintings 1 through 8. In the process of making the descriptions, the image of the woman is featured: the flesh-colored rose in the description is replaced by an image of a woman carrying a rose; she is given a name in paragraph 9. In another story, the murdered dressmaker's dummy provides the impulse for the presence of black-suited policemen.

5 / VISION, VISUALIZATION

The fishnets and skittle pins they carry, in both paintings and paragraphs, are as mysterious as the notion of murdering a dressmaker's dummy.

Paragraphs 11 and 16 use phrases that are the titles of paintings 8 and 13: "the difficult crossing" and "the idol." "The difficult crossing" is never precisely defined, but "the idol" is related to another story: three white eggs are in paragraph 12 and in painting 10, which precede and then produce the Phoenix, described in paragraphs 17 and 18 and depicted as an eagle in painting 13 and as a hawk in painting 16.

Another story concerns a man in a bowler hat who is a doctor. The doctor appears in paragraphs 13 and 14 and then reappears in paragraph 19. Later, after the "I" narrator has gone through a metamorphosis as a woman, there are descriptions in paragraphs 22 and through 24 of someone walking down city streets and then crossing a river over a bridge. These descriptions are visually related to the paintings in which a bowler-hatted man does the same thing: paintings 17 and 18.

The hot key image appears in three paintings—11, 12, and 14—and in a paragraph—15. By implication it is related to the fire images in paintings 14, 15, and 16, and, very tenuously, to the entrance of "I" into the theater and his meeting with the blonde, in paragraph 17.

The final painting and the final paragraph come together as mutually supportive descriptions. In the paragraph, "I" is in front of his window, and a large mirror reflects the house opposite, as if the outside of the room were part of his room's interior. In the painting, the window frame becomes a frame for the house front opposite; in this way, the house front becomes a painting that is part of the interior of the room with the window, canceling out the exterior. Both mirrors and windows change the visual relationships of interior/exterior.

In both paintings and paragraphs, a process of metonymy changes the images. One of the most important instances of this process is the connecting of stones, rocks, and eggs, which are all introduced in the first two sentences of the description in part 5. Thereafter, stones and eggs keep reappearing either in their own forms or as related to other images: landscapes, seashores, eggs as booby traps, and eggs as a source of the Phoenix and of a rebirth cycle. The first Magritte painting depicts a large falling rock, and rocks are part of paintings 2 and 3 and of other seashore scenes. Eggs in a nest and a burning egg appear in other paintings, and flying birds—eagles or hawks—are images related to the Phoenix.

Robbe-Grillet uses the rock image and its metonymic relationships as suggested in the falling-rock painting as a generator for his narrative descriptions, without subscribing to Magritte's meanings. In a letter to a physicist friend, Magritte commented on the rock image in "Le Chateau des Pyrénées":

> By confronting us with a massive rock in mid air—something we know cannot happen—we are somehow forced to wonder why doesn't the rock come plunging down into the sea? We know, of course, that it should. But *why* should it?
>
> What fails to happen in the painting reminds us of the mystery of what actually does happen in the real world.
>
> Space, time, and matter are dramatized here in suspended animation. The force of gravity, which we dismiss as commonplace in our daily lives, becomes powerful and awesome here. We can step on an ordinary stone any day without giving it a second thought, but the stone in the painting is compelling. The artist has made it extraordinary. It reminds us that all stones are extraordinary.[13]

In fact, he goes on to say, the whole world is extraordinary and must be comprehended before we think of it scientifically. Everything becomes magnified in his vision and then in his painting as a means of visual comprehension. We can't see the atoms and molecules, but he can make us feel how impressive our sensual receptors are.

Magritte's titles reflect another aspect of his internal visualization. "The titles of my paintings accompany them like the names of objects without illustrating or explaining them," he has said (203). Nevertheless many titles do reflect his own favorite ideas or literary references. "Le Chateau des Pyrénées" comes from the book *Visions of a Castle of the Pyrenees*, possibly by one of his favorite Gothic romance writers, Ann Radcliffe. (Some critics have

5 / VISION, VISUALIZATION 123

questioned her authorship.) As a form of metonymy, the personal reference to a source known to Magritte but not necessarily to us suggests the mystery as well as the commonplace origins of artistic inspirations; it further suggests the multitude of possible ideas that inspiration can generate.

Robbe-Grillet uses Magritte's titles and paintings as generators for his text with the same freedom of movement and meaning that Magritte used in his art. Robbe-Grillet goes even further in his reference-making by using self-reference. Within the period (approximately 1971 to 1975) during which he wrote and published *La Belle Captive* and *Topologie*, he was collaborating with Rauschenberg, Delvaux, and Hamilton, and parts of these works, along with parts of *La Belle Captive*, are used to construct *Topologie* as the ultimate landscape of his mental universe during that time. Many of the ambiguous phrases used in subsection 5 of *Fifth Space*, such as "already said," "mentioned earlier," and "already described," refer to those other collaborative texts. Robbe-Grillet was well aware that Magritte's references and iconography existed in a different realm of consciousness and came from a different store of memory and perception from his own realm of consciousness, as he perceived and used the paintings. It complicates a reader's response to have two consciousnesses coloring the work *La Belle Captive*, but the complication makes the game more provocative. Bruce Morrissette sees their collaboration in semiotic terms:

> Robbe-Grillet's use of materials from Magritte may be analyzed according to this system: the painter's subjects, objects, titles, and all aspects other than the picture itself may be seen or defined as a precode; the actual Magritte picture, let us say *Le Chateau des Pyrénées*, is the coded work chosen by Robbe-Grillet and transformed by and within his text into a post-code.[14]

There are other terms besides "code" that can be applied to the Magritte/Robbe-Grillet relationship, such as "mise-en-abyme" and "slipping meanings." In the mise-en-abyme technique, an image or story appears in miniaturized form within the frame story or image. The miniaturized version is self-contained, just as a motive in music is self-contained as a fragment of the theme or subject. There are a number of mise-en-abyme motives at work in

La Belle Captive. They reflect the themes and images often used by Magritte although here transformed by Robbe-Grillet: bowler-hatted men, fishnets, skittle pins, and roses. The rose, for instance, experiences a number of transformations of meaning. One meaning is "explained" in a letter Magritte wrote about the rose in painting 18, "La Boîte de Pandore":

> The presence of the rose next to the stroller signifies that wherever man's destiny leads him he is always protected by an element of beauty. The painter hopes that this man is heading for the most sublime place in his life. The rose's vividness corresponds to its important role (element of beauty). The approach of nightfall suits withdrawal, and the bridge makes us think something will be overcome.[15]

Whether this explanation was made by Magritte humorously or was intended to be very serious as an explanation of the symbolic meaning of the painting, Robbe-Grillet has used the painting to create a "slipping meaning" for this text. Meanings, he has said, change by a number of processes: "effraction . . . infraction, refraction, diffraction, rupture, serial or combinatory organizations, all challenging the total meaning that seeks to blend everything, the structure can only become fleetingly the place for a precarious, slipping meaning, always ready to collapse."[16]

The bowler-hatted man in the paragraphs of description preceding and accompanying the painting "La Boîte de Pandore" is performing actions similar to the actions in the painting: he is crossing a bridge at dusk. One paragraph describes the point on the bridge that he is approaching—where the level of water is reaching the vault of the arch—and as he walks on the bridge he is confronted by a child of about twelve, a seller of flowers, who offers him her last rose. He pays for the rose but does not take it, as he is repelled by the notion of any contact with her. Behind him, he hears the muffled sound of a large rock falling from a great distance into the river.

The large rose, perhaps as Magritte said, an element of beauty in life, is for Robbe-Grillet the message of Pandora: a warning for the future threatened by the wares of sellers of beauty. Or perhaps the bowler-hatted man is the mediocre man who is always repelled by messages of beauty. The voice of this narrator in the text transmutes the painting and even completes the mysterious image of the Chateau in the Pyrénées, the rock falling in the river. The original meaning of the large rock has slipped into something else by its connection with this narrator and with this painting image.

Finally, the title and the image of the whole work—*The Beautiful Captive*—tells us a great deal about both Magritte's and Robbe-Grillet's aesthetics of vision and creation.

The painting titled *La Belle Captive* and used in part 2 of the Magritte/Robbe-Grillet book *La Belle Captive* is a 1967 version of a painting made in 1949. The two paintings are similar but not the same. The title evokes Magritte's favorite mystery character, Fantomas, the hero of a number of films and paperback novels in the early years of this century. A beautiful captive was a standard theme in erotic mystery novels, but the painting itself is not erotic, nor is there even the appearance of a female beauty. The meaning, in its actual appearance in this painting, can perhaps be deduced from a statement Magritte made about the art of painting:

> I have found a new possibility things may have: that of *gradually* becoming something else—an object *melts* into an object other than itself. For instance, at certain spots the sky allows wood to appear.... [U]sing this means, I get pictures in which the eye "must think" in a way entirely different from the usual.[17]

The easel in this painting appears in other paintings by Magritte, all of which block off parts of the landscape by a frame or even by superimposing easel versions of landscapes onto other landscapes.

> This is how we see the world. We see it outside ourselves and at the same time we only have a representation of it in ourselves. In the same way, we sometimes situate in the past that which is happening in the present. Time and space thus lose the vulgar meaning that only daily experience takes into account.[18]

And in his turn, when considering the nature of the world and of art, Robbe-Grillet said, "Modern art is precisely this attempt to construct something that is related to this life that we have within us, which is perhaps more important than the other one, and which does not function in the same manner as the rational one."[19]

For Robbe-Grillet, the dream state is especially important as a way to discover the life within us, as well as the special kind of space within us. The state of dream and the sense of space particularly define his kinship-relationship with Magritte. Rather than using newspaper articles, gossip, or other real or invented forms of reality to nourish his imaginary life, as he has done in other works, Robbe-Grillet uses the pictorial inventions of life made by Magritte to stir up his own powers to "invent constantly the world" (47).

He had no desire at all to illustrate or in any way to clarify the visual images of Magritte's work; he wanted instead to use his text and Magritte's images to "play antagonistic roles" ... to "put the image in a state of crisis" (39). It was a game, he said, that could not in fact be completed since Magritte was dead and could not respond, but Robbe-Grillet complicated the game even more by using in part 2 of the book *La Belle Captive* (but not in *Topology*) something that he had written *earlier* as a beginning of another novel (not published) and then used again in his second assemblage novel *Souvenirs du triangle d'or* (1977–78). All the rest of the book *La Belle Captive* is used in *Souvenirs*, along with a previously collaborative work with Irina Ionesco (photographs and text), work previously done with Jasper Johns, and some never before published work of his own.

Since the segment used in part 2 of *La Belle Captive* was written without any conscious intention (it is supposed) of relating that text to the paintings of Rene Magritte, the result, directed by Robbe-Grillet's choice, is a pure coincidence of meaning, an example, as Bruce Morrissette calls it, of "surrealist hasard objectif."[20]

In both Robbe-Grillet's and Magritte's work, imagination never completely departs from a sensual experience of the real world. Precision of detail and thematic evocation of the "terrors" of the real world keep that world clearly in view. A sense of concreteness and of uneasy meaning comes through *La Belle Captive* in spite of the deliberate barriers to rational interpretation created by Robbe-Grillet.

Imagination is always presented as though it were the product of a consciousness (a narrator) in Robbe-Grillet's works, even in the deliberately fragmented, self-quoting, self-plagiarizing, art-inspired assemblage novels. In the other novels, the author and his transformations, presumably imaginative reconstructions of himself, appear as several consciousnesses (described in the third person), as "I"'s, or as passive voices.

The innovation in *Topology* is that, as several linked stories are told, several changes in the shape of the narrator are made. The protean narrative voice keeps the elements of the work linked, moving and changing in and out of states of mind and reality. The presence of a "voice" inflicts itself on the reader. Although Robbe-Grillet rejects the usual deception practiced on readers by conventional novels, he must have some connection. He is being read, and he seems to want to acknowledge that experience.

The Elusive Narrator

In *Incipit*, an "I" narrator describes a vision that he is experiencing in a condition close to sleep. In *First Space*, "Construction of a ruined temple to the goddess Vanadis," the "I" narrator describes omnisciently several places: a prison for juvenile courtesans, a ruined city used as a tourist attraction, and a mythological place, existing in 39 B.C., that was peopled by young girls who never got old and who were kept going as a population by their impregnation by a girl-king hermaphrodite. Description in *First Space* of places leads to story-telling, possibly by the "I" narrator. The story is transformed into a theatrical performance, and the narrator as an "I" has disappeared. Instead, a character named David, who is present at the theatrical performance, is remembering an event of thirty years before in which he ascended the "endless staircase of some vast abandoned building."[21] The *Space* concludes with his reactions to the performance.

In *Second Space*, "Ascending rehearsals for a motionless dwelling," David's memory or dream is described, in the third person. In the description, the word "possibly" is used, indicating that the describer is imagining the events but is not omniscient.

In *Third Space*, "Construction of a ruined temple (continued and concluded)," the narrator is an "I" who is involved in clearing up "a number of as yet imprecise or contradictory details, this without prejudice to their ultimate importance as regards the text as a whole" (69). This paragraph sounds like an author's notes for a future text; in the paragraph, he is a reporter of contemporary events. An archeological site is being cleared, and he is recording the clearing.

Immediately thereafter, the "I" narrator appears at a dress rehearsal of the play *David*, at which he meets several friends (one of them named Berg, as in Rauschenberg). He leaves the theater, but the next description is about the discovery of the body of a murdered girl at the theater, described as though he were present.

The discovery of another murdered girl and the discussion of the murder investigation is reported in the third person. When a building is discovered, the "I" narrator appears again, announcing that this building has in fact already been photographed; he identifies himself again as a reporter for the archeological team.

In *Fourth Space*, "Reveries of young girls confined between window and looking glass," the narration alternates between third person and first person. Occasionally the first person describes herself: "She who looks at herself for too long finds the glass has duplicated her. I see a second girl, the improbable lover, other, inaccessible, born of solitude and dream and of the venturing hand" (89). And another description is made in another style: "I am a studious little girl; I go to school every day, and no one waits for me when I come out of class" (91).

Fifth Space, "The criminal already on my trail," begins with "I remember" (107). The "I" narrator describes his walks through the city, ending each description with a return to sleep. The next part is third-person narration through what seems to be the point of view of a young girl, who is describing the events leading to her own murder. The following part is also third-person narration, describing a varied landscape: a Graeco-Roman temple, a black bull on a hill nearby, a deserted railway station, a locomotive, and a building, in the basement of which another murder is discovered. The scene shifts, in the next part of *Fifth Space*, to the interior of a building, which seems to be like the interior of the prison described in *First Space*. Under a trapdoor is a sacrificial altar to "Vanquished Vanadis" (125). Though the narration seems to be by

5 / VISION, VISUALIZATION

an omniscient third person, a number of phrases occur that once more express doubts or questions about the events: "hardly admits of speculation" (124); "apparently admitting daylight" (125); "this must be the outcome" (125); "Let us also quickly recall here" (126).

The next part of *Fifth Space* becomes again description by an "I" narrator, who recounts his own actions in detail, including his brief metamorphosis as a woman. *Fifth Space* concludes with a description by an "I" narrator of himself in a room. He is sitting in front of a window, and a mirror is reflecting the exterior of the house opposite. Compositionally, he is part of the picture, and he is working imaginatively—"laboriously reconstructing the plan ... day after day" of what he calls a "fanatic temple" (138).

The structure, though not the meaning, of *Topology* is resolved in the *Coda*. It begins with the sound of a cry, a sound that has previously occurred: at the beginning of *Incipit*, at the end of the first part of *First Space*, in the title of the third part of *Fifth Space*. This final version of the structure recognizes all the themes and motifs and uses them.

Coda: A Drawing Together

The "I" narrator awakens and mentally projects himself ("I remember now" [139]) into what he calls the "impossibly large dwelling" (139) that stands in the middle of a forest. Describing it (satirically) as "once peopled ... by the convenient theory of small minor deities" (139–40), the narrator moves through it in "my spiraling way" (140).

The description then shifts, in the next paragraph, to images of butterflies and a moth hunter. Only an ellipsis has indicated a break in the text and a new direction. The following four paragraphs are concerned with butterflies, or what he calls "vanessas [a genus of butterfly] or iridescent goddesses" (140–41). In the last of the four paragraphs, the butterflies are "sacrificed," recalling the murders called sacrifices of the young girls described in earlier parts of the book. The goddess to whom they are sacrificed is called "Voluptuous Vanadis (also known as the Vampire

Vanadis)" (141), recalling the hermaphrodite god of the myth earlier described.

Three of the four paragraphs begin with the same image: "[t]here was *blood* under the half-open door" (140); "[n]ow the *red pool* is spreading over the checkered paving of the long corridor" (140); "[a]nd the red blood runs in a vermilion rivulet that will soon pass through the dark chink beneath the ill-fitting door, etc." (141). The final description of the blood under the door is followed by a sentence describing a sea and sandy beach, with beached shellfish and kelp on the shore. Blood and water blend by this descriptive juxtaposition, but (still following the metonymic process that Robbe-Grillet has used throughout this book) they suggest each other but are not symbolically the same. They both flow, they both are related to life and death, but blood is part of the sacrifice images used, and the wave is cleansing, washing everything away.

Another motif from previous parts of *Topology* is the shoe, which recalls the image as it has been used in "A double-backed altar." Shoes have been used in many Robbe-Grillet novels, and their presence here evokes loss or metamorphosis: "the delicate abandoned slipper lying on its side ... during one of those hasty, half-conscious undressing operations" becomes in the following sentence "[t]he little iridescent goddesses make such unexpected, rapid movements that one barely sees their transformations take place" (141). The abandoned slipper has a number of suggestions—abandoned clothing on a seashore and drowning, the abandoned pupa of a butterfly, Cinderella's abandoned slipper.

A final motif is the house image with which the *Coda* concludes: "And I move on, yet again, faced with the row of closed doors, down the endless empty corridor, unalterably neat and clean" (142). The *Coda* began with the image of the abandoned house in the forest, and it concludes with this image of emptiness and searching in a house with many rooms. Magritte's painting *Le Chateau des Pyrénnées*, the first image in the book *La Belle Captive*, and the first description in part 5, *Space Fifth* of *Topology*, is a chateau on a huge rock falling through the air, or flying, with an implication of sea and sand below. This startling image could be the generator for most of the motifs used in the final section, the

Coda. It is visionary and suggestive, precise in its details but fantastic in its probability. It suggests myth but not the purpose or form of the myth. It suggests dream and fantasy, and there are many dreams and fantasies described in the book, disturbing dreams and fantasies of sexual violence and cultural violence. But is the novel ideological? Ronald Bogue in "Meaning and Ideology in Robbe-Grillet's *Topologie d'une cité fantôme*" says that Robbe-Grillet cannot avoid ideology. Formal analysis is incomplete in dealing with Robbe-Grillet:

> [He] can protest the ideological codification of reality, which promotes one social group's domination of another, by deforming bourgeois myths and thereby displaying the arbitrary nature of their formation. ... Robbe-Grillet ... disassembles myths and restructures their elements in accordance with a metacritical analysis of the ideology implicit in these myths which is communicated by the texts and forms part of their meaning.[22]

Robbe-Grillet, he says, like other contemporary theoreticians, is "obsessed by the question of what constitutes political, linguistic, and sexual freedom" and his obsession "finds expression in *Topology*" (43). "Protest" and "obsession" are strong words to use in describing Robbe-Grillet's use of aspects of contemporary reality; these are words that imply commitment or, as Bogue insists "a strategy to remake the world after his desires" (42). So much of Robbe-Grillet's artistic energy and thinking processes were involved in creating this novel—five years, according to him in an interview[23]—that it is difficult to believe that ideology and commitment were central or immediate concerns. His constant exchanges with the artists David Hamilton, Paul Delvaux, and Robert Rauschenberg show his fascination with connections between word and picture rather than between reality and reconstruction of reality:

> I proposed written images to them and they offered me pictorial images: photographs from Hamilton, prints from Rauschenberg, and engravings from Delvaux. And each time as I went along, the elements they furnished me through their images were integrated into my text. Then I would send them the text which they in turn reinte-

grated into their own work. . . . [F]or the first time I wanted the generators to be completely external, that is for them to be supplied by others who spoke to me and whose sensitivity was often close to mine on certain points. (230)

These exchanges of perceptions—without intellectual discussion, without refusal or argument, without qualification—if they occurred as Robbe-Grillet has described, are extraordinary instances of collaboration between writer and artist. They engender the works in truly parental fashion, allowing a mingling of personal elements that creates an entity that lives on its own. Though he has admitted that there are elements from his films G*lissements progressifs du plaisir* and *Le jeu avec le feu* (both made while he was working on *Topology*) that appear in the novel, this self-generation complicates but does not interfere with the free movement of his exchanges.

It is the free movement in the engendering of the text, in the multiplication of sources, the acceptance of suggestions, that makes ideological or precisely theoretical interpretation of Robbe-Grillet's works problematic. He is not averse to interpretation, but he delights in subverting it. The voice of the subjective, protean narrator, with his doubts and hesitations, his confusions and his humor, clearly a narrative part of *Topology*, emanates from the head of this author, who is presenting himself in a different form from past conventions of the "author," conventions that have been challenged by several contemporary critics.

6
Author? Author

Challenging the importance of the author leaves the work of art very vulnerable, but critics Michel Foucault and Roland Barthes want the text to be without defenses, open completely to a reader's interpretation.

"Using all the contrivances that he sets up between himself and what he writes, the writing subject cancels out the signs of his particular individuality," Foucault declares. "[W]hat difference does it make who is speaking?"[1]

"The removal of the Author ... utterly transforms the modern text (or—which is the same thing—the text is henceforth made and read in such a way that at all its levels the author is absent)," says Barthes.[2]

Foucault is fearful of the author and his meanings, and he wishes for "a form of culture in which fiction would not be limited by the figure of the author."[3] Barthes wishes to dispense with the author in order to make room for the reader: "[A] text is made of multiple writings, drawn from many cultures and entering into mutual relations of dialogue, parody, contestation, but there is one place where this multiplicity is focused and that place is the reader, not ... the author. ... [A] text's unity lies not in its origin but in its destination."[4] The silent, modest presence of the author (grudgingly conceded by these critics) has only a limited influence on the product he produces, which enjoys its complete fulfillment when it is consumed by the reader. The language of the marketplace is appropriate, for this reader, in considering the implications of these views, i.e., the text as vegetable is fulfilled when it is consumed by the shopper, who buys without regard for the earth, the farmer, the tools that brought it to fruition. This disregard for and even suspicion of the author as artist, denying him/her a presence or an active persona except as a compiler of cultural diversity, is not the same as the idea of the artist expressed by critic-philosopher Georg Lukacs:

> The creating of the artist is the only case in the whole of being where one human subject, having become purified but still remaining subjective-personal, can produce beyond himself. . . . The paradox of esthetic value-realization is that it *is inseparably bound to the personality either as a path or as a goal* [my italics]; but that which comes from this personality into the work separates itself definitively from the generative subject, has nothing more to do with him, and stands there before him as a being fulfilled in itself and unattainable.[5]

There is a writer, a reader, and a work, and each one may at some time stand alone as an entity with a purpose in itself, *but also as a necessary triad for the experience of reading*. For Wolfgang Iser, the "act of reading" is the whole goal and requires a reconsideration of the "time-honored opposition" of fiction and reality, replacing such an opposition with "the concept of communication,"[6] firmly including the roles of the reader and the author. In such communication, the concern is with the effect of the text and not its meaning. How does the act of reading work? Iser summarizes it in this way:

> Let us sum up our findings so far: fictional language has the basic properties of the illocutionary act.[7] It relates to conventions which it carries with it, and it also entails procedures which, in the form of strategies, help to guide the reader to an understanding of the selective processes underlying the text. It has the quality of "performance," in that it makes the reader produce the code governing this selection as the actual meaning of the text. With its horizontal organization of different conventions, and its frustration of established expectations, it takes on an *illocutionary force*, and the potential effectiveness of this not only arouses attention but also guides the reader's approach to the text and elicits responses to it. (61–62)

Since the illocutionary act has force (it orders, warns, undertakes, etc.), it cannot do without a force source, or an author. Robbe-Grillet may cancel out the signs of his own individuality in his texts, but he does not eliminate himself. He is very much the organizer and unifier of his work, whose "head" (ideas and emotions) gets in the way of the viewer's sight and whose humors and whimsies propose images and interpretations in his works that transcend an expected re-creation of reality. He does not acquiesce in his own death because he remains the reader's guide through the scenes and images he has chosen. The term "ghosts" in the translation of his first "autobiography" does describe the persistent haunting of the self by memories and fantasies, and the writer as guide is an elusive, uneasy, and mysterious presence in his work, but Robbe-Grillet's ghosts do not disintegrate or become unnecessary. They are always present in the relationship between the writer and his work. They are all products of one subjectivity, and a subjectivity does not declare its individuality or personality. It does not analyze itself nor is it subject to analysis by an internal narrator. For the purposes of the immediate experience of reading, the subjectivity has the reader in his/her power.

The Writer and the Real

Alain Robbe-Grillet's novel writing and filmmaking demand that he use his imagination actively and freely. Imagination, for him, is the key to genuine advances in art, and through imaginative freedom in experimentation, he says, "[T]he discovery of reality will continue."[8] Since all artists aspire to discover reality, reality has taken different forms and has had different meanings through the ages; as each artist "abandon(ed) outworn forms" (ibid.), he/she discovered the reality that constituted his/her personal reality. Thus art advanced. Artistic reality is not constant. It cannot be measured against an absolute model of life; the forms and truths of life itself change through the ages and in the eyes of human beings. The novel is a form of exploration:

> It never knows what it is seeking; it is ignorant of what it has to say; it is invention, invention of the world and of men, constant invention and perpetual interrogation. (161)

The creator's problem, Robbe-Grillet says, is to *seek* the truth,[9] which he can only do by means of his own relations with reality. His relations with reality produce meanings that are tentative and provisional:

> There remains, then, that immediate signification of things (descriptive, partial, always contested)—in other words, the signification which takes place within the story, the anecdote of the book.... It is on this immediate signification that the effort of exploration and creation will henceforth be brought to bear.[10]

For him, the story, or the "anecdote," of the book will be an experiment in storytelling; the story will mean only what it needs to mean in the context of the work. Because the story does not have to relate to life or to point up some absolute truth in life, it is highly manipulable. However, for Robbe-Grillet, the elements and sources of the story are always derived from real life:

> [M]y relations with realism are not simple. I think there is a constant tension in my books between a sort of ideal abstraction to which I give voice, and, despite everything, the sort of empirical reality we find in novels in the last century ... unresolved tensions between two poles, a tension between the subjective and the objective, the realist illusion and total abstraction, and between the erotic which functions as such and another which would be impossible within the domain of the erotic ... tension between the personal and the impersonal.[11]

Totally realistic writing would be totally objective; totally imaginative writing would be totally subjective. Robbe-Grillet's sources have objective reality, and his impersonal tone seems to be objective. His goals are subjective. He separates, combines, and looks at his realities as imaginatively as possible, and in the process attacks his sources: "Any work of art destroys the reality before us and recreates it"[12]

In any Robbe-Grillet work, realistic images (objects, people, places) are created briefly for our immediate mental and visual perceptions, but they never come alive enough to exist independently of his story in our imaginations and speculations. The woman in *L'Immortelle*, the protagonist in *The Man Who Lies*, Wallas in *The Erasers* are sharply formed when they are present to our perceptions, but they are deliberately put out of action at the end of the story in which they appear. Robbe-Grillet does not aspire to create living forms. Like the surrealists, Robbe-Grillet constantly challenges man's capacity for change and for taking a chance:

> [M]an is that animal who at each moment invents other creative possibilities, other possible pieces of information, in a world which appears to become inert at every moment.[13]

Unlike the surrealists, change for Robbe-Grillet is not primarily social change. He is not interested in revolutionary activity nor does he believe that artists can change the world. However, he does believe that he can "make the gear wheels" of established society "grind":

> [I try to] work against ideology on the one hand by pointing it out, and on the other hand in making it grind so that it can be heard, so that it will not be innocent . . . [or] natural. (19)

A highly conscious withdrawal from the political and social revolution and an insistence on the need for a revolution in consciousness define the limits of Robbe-Grillet's iconoclasm. On one hand, he cannot join revolutionary groups or parties, but on the other hand, he can challenge consciousness without submitting to his unconscious. Like the surrealists, Robbe-Grillet welcomes accident and other previously unplanned elements into his work, but unlike them, he acknowledges his fellow believers but works alone and is wary of any theory, even his own, that might circumscribe his work.

The Slipping Relationship between Theory and Practice in Alain Robbe-Grillet's Creative Work

> I am, myself, very allergic to the concept of truth, as you know, and if I like a theory, it is only as long as it does not become a dogma, as long as it does not pretend to be the truth.[14]

As is true in general, the relationship between theory and practice in an artist's work is not perfect, but the work does not have to be justified or found wanting on the basis of its relationship to expressed ideas. Perhaps his disclaimer about dogma has a self-serving function, but Robbe-Grillet's many ideas about art and about his perception of his own art raise questions instead of giving answers. No single theory about what novels or films should be is stated in his essays or interviews; no single conviction about the nature of reality is affirmed.

The closest to an all-encompassing explanation of his methods is in the statement that he wants to "displace things in relation to their normal position ... [creating] a shifting order."[15] Yet such a statement does not confront the issue of what "normal" position is. The following passage is a good example of his obliqueness in explaining both normal and abnormal:

> I had formulated all the meaning possible (the structure, when it was formulated, was already of meaning), and the text began precisely at that moment, at the moment when the theory had pushed the meaning as far as possible and when there would have to be something unthinkable about to happen. This would not be established meaning, nor new meaning, nor changing and plural meaning, nor even produced meaning which was ignorant of its own potential, but a meaning which would declare itself to be impossible.[16]

What Robbe-Grillet seems to be saying is that theory can initiate a structure for a work, but then that structure is freed up, and an "impossible" (to predict?) text is born. The text is the Phoenix, perhaps because for the artist the completed work is always a new and amazing creation that he/she never could have imagined producing. This concept of inspiration and production is like the surrealist idea of creation: "They [the surrealists] threw themselves into the dark recesses of being. . . . 'Illumination' comes afterward."[17] Robbe-Grillet has shifted his emphases as he has enlarged on his ideas. In the early writings in the 1950s and 1960s, he made an issue of the precise surface nature of his descriptions, the impersonality of a kind of description that made the objects described visible in themselves and not as anthropomorphic forms containing the emotions of their creators. In his later theories and assemblage works, he has cut up the pieces of description like a rather perverse creator of puzzles. His subjective responses to his material are visible everywhere, and he confirms his subjectivity in his autobiography/romanesques—*Le Miroir qui revient (Ghosts in the Mirror)*, 1985, *Angélique ou l'enchantement*, 1988, and *Les Derniers Jours de Corinthe*, 1994. In fact, he seems still to be exploring the possibilities of response. It is Robbe-Grillet who is responding to the labyrinth idea, or to the forest in the Carpathians, or to the myths of heroes. It is Robbe-Grillet who is fascinated by archeological levels of reality and by the interplay between visual art and language. His aesthetic emotions control his labors.

As an artist, Robbe-Grillet is not inconsistent. He began by looking into the possibilities of expressing subjectivity while seeming to be objective in descriptions without emotion, and he has transformed his explorations into some form of self-exploration. Part of his reluctance to be labeled and defined by theory, particularly other people's theory, comes from his irritation with the idea of absolute truth: "[T]he ensemble of my novels and films is precisely opposed to the notion of fixed truth."[18]

His most recent statements, tackling the idea of political correctness (and, implicitly, the accusations against him of treating women as objects), reject the idea that the artist can be "correct." The writer writes for himself and against himself, alone; he can only be correct or incorrect with himself. He is only an individual and not a representative of the majority or the minority. He is of course a product of the ideology of his culture, but he, Robbe-Grillet, has always tried to write *against ideology*, against what he is expected to accept and feel.[19]

His defensiveness is understandable, since as an artist he has exposed his imagination and his particular proclivities and cannot reject them. Though he has remained his essential *self*, he has experimented with the possibilities of novel and film form more than almost any other writer of this century. His experiments cannot be ignored or dismissed. Surely his work will be there as a conscious or unconscious model for the art of the future.

Notes

Introduction

1. Erich Auerbach, *Mimesis: The Representation of Reality in Western Literature* (Princeton: Princeton University Press, 1968), 491.

2. Letter to Guy de Maupassant (1870), in Gustave Flaubert, *Letters*, ed. Richard Rumbold, trans. J. M. Cohen (London: George Weidenfelt and Nicholson Ltd., 1950), 218.

3. Richard Wollheim, "Art and Illusion," in *Aesthetics in the Modern World*, ed. Harold Osborne (New York: Weybright and Talley, 1968), 236.

4. Maurice Merleau-Ponty, "The Primacy of Perception," in *The Primacy of Perception and other essays*, ed. James M. Edie (Evanston: Northwestern University Press, 1964), 34.

5. Stephen Heath, *The Nouveau Roman: A Study in the Practice of Writing* (London: Elek, 1977), 99.

6. Alain Robbe-Grillet, "Nature, Humanism, and Tragedy," in *For a New Novel*, trans. Richard Howard (New York: Grove Press, 1965), 49–75.

7. John Sturrock, *The French New Novel* (London: Oxford University Press, 1969), 5.

8. See also Henri Micciollo, *"La Jalousie" d'Alain Robbe-Grillet* (Paris: Librairie Hachette, 1972).

9. Bruce Morrissette, *The Novels of Robbe-Grillet* (Ithaca: Cornell University Press, 1975), 37.

10. Jean Alter, *La Vision du monde d'Alain Robbe-Grillet: structures et significations* (Genève: Librairie Droz, 1966), 37.

11. Alain Robbe-Grillet, "The French New Novel," trans. Anna Otten, *Antioch Review* 47 (summer 1987): 200.

12. Quoted by Barry Chabot, "The Problem of the Postmodern," in Ingeborg Hoesterey, ed., *Zeitgeist in Babel: The Postmodernist Controversey* (Bloomington and Indianapolis: Indiana University Press, 1991), 25.

13. Terry Eagleton, "Capitalism, Modernism and Postmodernism," in David Lodge, ed., *Modern Criticism and Theory, A Reader* (London and New York: Longman, 1988), 386.
14. Frederic Jameson, *Postmodernism or the Cultural Logic of Late Capitalism* (Durham: Duke University Press, 1991), xxii .
15. Victor Shlovsky, "Art as technique," in Lodge, *Modern Criticism and Theory,* 25.
16. Wolfgang Iser, "The reading process: a phenomenological approach," in Lodge, *Modern Criticism and Theory*, 212–27.
17. Judi Freeman, *Mark Tansey Catalogue,* Los Angeles County Museum of Art (San Francisco: Chronicle Books , 1993), 37.
18. Alain Robbe-Grillet, *Ghosts in the Mirror,* trans. Jo Levy (New York: Grove Weidenfeld, 1988), 44.
19. *Le Miroir qui revient*, 1985; *Angélique ou l'enchantement*, 1988; *Les Derniers Jours de Corinthe*, 1994.
20. Alain Robbe-Grillet, "A Graveyard of Identities and Uniforms," trans. Stewart Spencer, in Freeman, *Mark Tansey Catalogue*, 7.
21. Robbe-Grillet, *Ghosts in the Mirror*, 159.
22. Ronald Siegel, "Hallucinations," in *The Mind's Eye: Readings from Scientific American* (New York: W. H. Freeman and Company, 1976–86), 109.
23. Georg Lukács, "On the Phenomenology of the Creative Process," *The Philosophical Forum* (Department of Philosophy, Boston University) 3.3–4 (spring–summer 1972–73): 321.
24. For an analysis of Robbe-Grillet's ludic structures and his ties to other arts, see Ben Stoltzfus, *Alain Robbe-Grillet: The Body of the Text* (Cranbury, N.J.: Associated University Presses, 1985).

Chapter One: Origins and Attitudes: Robbe-Grillet States His Beliefs

1. Alain Robbe-Grillet, *For a New Novel: Essays on Fiction,* trans. Richard Howard (New York: Grove Press, 1965), 77–78.
2. "Enigmas and Transparency in Raymond Roussel," 86.
3. "Zeno's Sick Conscience," 94.
4. "Joë Bousquet the Dreamer," 95–109.
5. "Samuel Beckett or Presence on the Stage," 128.
6. "A Novel that Invents Itself," 128.
7. "From Realism to Reality," 161.
8. Alain Robbe-Grillet, *Glissements progressifs du plaisir,* ciné-roman (Paris: Les Editions du Minuit, 1974), 12–13.
9. Alain Robbe-Grillet, "Order and Disorder in Film and Fiction," trans. Bruce Morrissette, *Critical Inquiry* 4.1 (autumn 1977): 19.

10. Alain Robbe-Grillet, "Sur le choix de générateurs," in *Colloque de Cérisy, nouveau roman: hier, aujourd'hui, 2. Pratiques, Jean Ricardou*, ed. (Paris: Union Générale d'Editions, 1972), 160.

11. André Gardies, ed., "Alain Robbe-Grillet: Textes et Documents," in *Cinéma d'aujourd'hui 70* (Paris: Edition Seghers, 1972), 115.

12. Alain Robbe-Grillet, with photographs by David Hamilton, *Les Demoiselles* (Paris: Les Editions de Minuit, 1973); trans. Martha Egan, *Sisters* (New York: Morrow, 1973). Alain Robbe-Grillet and René Magritte, *La Belle Captive* (Paris: La Bibliothèque Des Arts, 1976); trans. Ben Stoltzfus (Berkeley: University of California Press, 1995).

13. Bruce Morrissette, "Robbe-Grillet at the University of Chicago," *French Review* 50.1 (October 1976): 655–57.

14. Jean Ricardou, ed.., *Colloque de Cérisy, Alain Robbe-Grillet, I Roman/Cinéma* (Paris: Union Générale d'Editions, 1976), 420–21.

15. Gardies, "Alain Robbe-Grillet: Textes et Documents," 105.

16. Ronald Bogue, "Meaning and Ideology in Robbe-Grillet's *Topologie d'une cité fantôme*," *Modern Language Studies* 14.1 (winter 1984): 34.

17. Susan Suleiman, "Reading Robbe-Grillet: Sadism and Text in *Projet pour une révolution à New York*," *Romanic Revue* 68 (January 1977): 49.

18. Alain Robbe-Grillet, *Ghosts in the Mirror*, trans. Jo Levy (New York: Grove Weidenfeld, 1988), 5.

19. Jenny Weil, "A Talk with Alain Robbe-Grillet," *The New Leader* 55.15 (24 July 1972): 14.

20. Alain Robbe-Grillet, *L'Année dernière à Marienbad* (Paris: Les Editions de Minuit, 1961), 16.

21. Robbe-Grillet, "Order and Disorder in Film and Fiction," 16.

22. Wolfgang Iser, "The reading process: a phenomenological approach," in *Modern Criticism and Theory* (London and New York: Longman, 1988), 227.

Chapter 2: Confused and Misled: The Narrator Takes Part in an Old Myth

1. Alain Robbe-Grillet, *The Erasers*, trans. Richard Howard (New York: Grove Press, 1962), 7. In this chapter, all further quotations from and references to *The Erasers* are from this edition and are cited parenthetically in the text.

2. "[C]e sont des gommes dans le cerveau" (These are gummed up works [or erasers] in the brain). Comment by Robbe-Grillet in *Colloque de Cérisy, Robbe-Grillet 2. Cinéma/Roman* (Paris: Union Genérale d'Editions, 1976), 421.

3. Alain Robbe-Grillet, *Les Gommes* (Paris: Les Editions de Minuit, 1953), 15–16.

4. Wolfgang Iser, *The Act of Reading: A Theory of Aesthetic Response* (Baltimore: Johns Hopkins University Press, 1978), 19.

5. The play quality of Robbe-Grillet's work is discussed in the collection of essays *Robbe-Grillet and the Fantastic*, ed. Virginia Harger-Grinling and Tony

Chadwick (Westport, Conn.: Greenwood Press, 1994), and André Gardies, "Vers un mode de rapport nouveau avec le spectator: le ludique," in *Cahiers du 20ieme siècle: cinéma et littérature* (Paris: Editions Klincksieck, 1978), 93–102.

6. Alain Robbe-Grillet, *Ghosts in the Mirror*, trans. Jo Levy (New York: Grove Weidenfeld, 1988), 29–30.

7. Ralph Yarrow, "Traces of the Trickster," in Harger-Grinling and Chadwick, *Robbe-Grillet and the Fantastic*, 38.

Chapter 3: The Hidden I and the Camera Eye: Novels and a Film Re-Create Obsession

1. Roland Barthes, "Objective Literature: Alain Robbe-Grillet," introductory essay in *Two Novels by Robbe-Grillet,* trans. by Richard Howard (New York: Grove Press, 1965), 21. Reprinted from *Evergreen Review* 5 (summer 1958).

2. Alain Resnais and Alain Robbe-Grillet, *Evolution d'une écriture* (Paris: Lettres Modernes, Menard, 1974).

3. Alain Robbe-Grillet, writer and director, *L'Immortelle* (*The Immortal One*) (Istanbul, 1963); also made into a ciné-roman (Paris: Les Editions de Minuit, 1963). Robbe-Grillet is not the inventor of the ciné-roman form. "[He] has revived and refined the *ciné-roman* [film-novel] from the abstract justifications of the cinema as an art form for which Louis Deluc first used the term" (William F. van Wert, *The Film Career of Alain Robbe-Grillet* (Pleasantville, N.Y.: Redgrave Publishing Co., 1977), 8.

4. Alain Robbe-Grillet, *The Immortal One*, trans. A. M. Sheridan Smith (London: Calder and Boyars, 1971), 7.

5. *L'Immortelle* took form in Robbe-Grillet's visual imagination before it took the concrete form of the scenario. To some extent, he has said, the concreteness of the scenario made him aware of the dangers of predetermined form for his creative ideas. See André Gardies, ed., "Alain Robbe-Grillet: Textes et Documents," in *Cinéma d'aujourd'hui 70* (Paris: Editions Seghers, 1972), 120. These ideas were also expressed in *Obliques*, the Robbe-Grillet issue, 16–17 (September 1978): 152.

6. Page numbers and shot numbers are from the *ciné-roman*. According to Robbe-Grillet, the shot numbers were given in the *ciné-roman* exactly as they were used in the final filmed work (*The Immortal One*, 5). The shot descriptions used here are all quotations; the sound descriptions that parallel the shot descriptions are my observations.

7. Jean Ricardou, ed., *Colloque de Cérisy, Robbe-Grillet, I, Roman/Cinéma* (Paris: Union Générale d'Editions, 1976), 173–213.

8. Robbe-Grillet, *The Immortal One*, 39.

9. The film glossary that follows this section has definitions of all the terms used here.

10. Lillian Dumont and Sandra Silverberg, "An Interview with Alain Robbe-Grillet," *French Review* 50.4 (March 1977): 653.

11. "Jules Michelet's *La Sorcière* was the inspiration for the protagonist Alice in *Glissements*," says Robbe-Grillet. "She and the Sorcière are both free spirits who defy social conventions. Society attempts, unsuccessfully, to punish them" (ibid., 654).

12. Stephen Heath, *The Nouveau Roman: A Study in the Practice of Writing* (London: Elek, 1977), 100.

Chapter 4: Perception and Deception: *The Man Who Lies* and *Djinn*

1. The film was made on location in Czechoslovakia at the chateau of the Baroness von Czobel. William R. van Wert, *The Film Career of Alain Robbe-Grillet* (Pleasantville, N.Y.: Redgrave Publishing Co., 1977), 30–33.

2. Michel Fano, "Projet sonore final (première bobine)," *Obliques* 16–17 (September 1978): 181–82.

3. André Gardies, ed., "Alain Robbe-Grillet: Textes et Documents," in *Cinéma d'aujourd'hui 70* (Paris: Editions Seghers, 1972), 134.

4. Jean Ricardou, ed., *Colloque de Cérisy, Robbe-Grillet, 2, Cinéma/Roman*, "Géographie de Robbe-Grillet," Tom Bishop (Paris, Union Générale d'Editions, 1976), 52–67.

5. Maurice Merleau-Ponty, *Phenomenology of Perception*, trans. Colin Smith (New York: Humanities Press, 1962), 294.

6. Ricardou, ed., *Colloque de Cérisy, Robbe-Grillet, 2*. Discussion of Tom Bishop talk, Robbe-Grillet comment, 78.

7. Gardies, ed., *Cinéma d'aujourd'hui 70*, Robbe-Grillet comment, 122.

8. Ricardou, ed., *Colloque de Cérisy, 2*, Robbe-Grillet comment, 72.

9. Ibid.

10. An intertextual relationship is with the film *Glissements progressifs du plaisir*, 1974, in which the heroine's name is Alice. The names *Boris* and *Jean* are persistently used in Robbe-Grillet's works: *Un régicide, Les gommes, Le maison de rendezvous* (very briefly), *Djinn, Eden et après, Trans-europ-express*.

11. Gardies, ed., *Cinéma d'aujourd'hui 70*, 145–48.

12. Ibid., 146.

13. Ricardou, ed., *Colloque de Cérisy, 2*, 128–29.

14. Gardies, ed., *Cinéma d'aujourd'hui 70*, 132.

15. Ricardou, ed., *Colloque de Cérisy, 2*, comment by Dominique Chateau during discussion following André Gardies' lecture, "Recit et materiau filmique," 124.

16. Susanne Langer, "On Significance in Music," in *Philosophy in a New Key* (New York: New American Library, 1951), 206–7.

17. Virginia Harger-Grinling and Tony Chadwick, eds., *Robbe-Grillet and the Fantastic: A Collection of Essays* (Westport, Conn.: Greenwood Press, 1994).
18. Alain Robbe-Grillet, *Djinn*, trans. Yvone Lenard and Walter Wells (New York: Grove Press, 1982), 106.
19. David Lodge, ed., *Modern Criticism and Theory*, Roland Barthes, "The death of the author" (London and New York: Longman, 1988), 167.
20. Alain Robbe-Grillet, *Ghosts in the Mirror*, trans. Jo Levy (New York: Grove Weidenfeld, 1988), 5.

Chapter 5: Vision, Visualization

1. Bruce Morrissette, *Intertextual Assemblage in Robbe-Grillet from Topology to the Golden Triangle* (Fredericton, N.B., Canada: York Press, 1979), 7.
2. Wallace Fowlie, *Age of Surrealism* (Bloomington: Indiana University Press, 1972), 33.
3. Ferdinand Alquié, *The Philosophy of Surrealism*, trans. B. Waldrop (Ann Arbor: The University of Michigan Press, 1969), 163.
4. Morrissette, *Intertextual Assemblage*, 79–80.
5. Lucy Lippard, ed. *Surrealists on Art* (Englewood Cliffs, N.J.: Prentice Hall, Inc., 1970), 2–3.
6. Willi Apel, *Harvard Dictionary of Music* (Cambridge: Harvard University Press, 1967), 353.
7. Webster's *New International Dictionary of the English Language*, 2nd ed., unabridged (Springfield, Mass.: G. and C. Merriam Company, 1950), 2670.
8. Quoted by Françoise Meltzer, "Preliminary Excavations of Robbe-Grillet's Phantom City," *Chicago Review* 28 (summer 1976): 41–50, referred to by Bruce Morrissette in "Post-Modern Generative Fiction: Novel and Film," *Critical Inquiry* 2.2 (winter 1975): 252–62.
9. Alain Robbe-Grillet, "Joë Bousquet, the Dreamer," in *For a New Novel* (New York: Grove Press, 1965), 97.
10. Alain Robbe-Grillet, *Topology of a Phantom City* (New York: Grove Press, 1977), 11.
11. Morrissette, *Intertextual Assemblage*, 17, quoting Jeanine Warnod, "Paul Delvaux—Alain Robbe-Grillet," *Le Figaro Littéraire*, 5 avril 1975, 5.
12. Alain Robbe-Grillet and René Magritte, *La Belle Captive*, roman (Lausanne-Paris: La Bibliothèque des Arts, 1975); the illustrations are courtesy of Mme. Georgette Magritte, Bruxelles.
13. Harry Torczyner, *Magritte, Ideas, and Images*, trans. Richard Miller (New York: Harry N. Abrams, Inc., 1977), 154.
14. Morrissette, *Intertextual Assemblage*, 78.
15. Torczyner, letter to Mr. & Mrs. Barnet Hodes, 1957, in Torczyner, *Magritte*, 90.

16. Robbe-Grillet, *Glissements progressifs du plaisir* (Paris: Les Editions de Minuit, 1974), 13. My translation.

17. Letter to Paul Nouge, 1927, in Torczyner, *Magritte*, 213.

18. Ibid., 156.

19. Robbe-Grillet, *Topology of a Phantom City*, 52.

20. David Leach, "Robbe-Grillet, 'Image and Texts: a dialogue,'"in *Generative Literature and Generative Art: New Essays* (Fredericton: N.B., Canada: York Press, 1993), 46.

21. Morrissette, *Intertextual Assemblage*, 45.

22. Ronald Bogue, "Meaning and Ideology in Robbe-Grillet's Topologie d'une cité fantôme," *Modern Language Studies* 14.1 (winter 1984): 34.

23. Beverly Langston, "Interview with Alain Robbe-Grillet," *Yale French Studies* 57 (1979): 228–37.

Chapter 6: Author? Author

1. Michel Foucault, "What Is an Author?" in *Modern Criticism and Theory, a Reader*, ed. David Lodge (London and New York: Longman, 1988), 198, 210.

2. Roland Barthes, "The Death of the Author," in *Modern Criticism and Theory*, op cit., 169.

3. Foucault, "What Is an Author?" 209.

4. Barthes, "The Death of the Author," 172.

5. Georg Lukaçs, "On the Phenomenology of the Creative Process," in *Philosophical Forum* (Boston University Dept. of Philosophy) 3.3–4 (spring 1972): 324–25.

6. Wolfgang Iser, *The Act of Reading; A Theory of Aesthetic Response* (Baltimore and London: Johns Hopkins University Press, 1978), passim.

7. J. L. Austin, "[W]e also perform *illocutionary acts* such as informing, ordering, warning, understating, etc., i.e., utterances which have a certain (conventional) force," quoted in Iser, *The Act of Reading*, 57.

8. Alain Robbe-Grillet, "From Realism to Reality (1955 and 1963)," in *For a New Novel*, trans. Richard Howard (New York: Grove Press, 1965), 158.

9. Statement in a lecture by Robbe-Grillet at the Carpenter Center for the Visual Arts, Harvard University, spring 1976, after a showing of the film *The Man Who Lies*.

10. Robbe-Grillet, "From Realism to Reality," 168. A similar comment is in the essay "New Novel, New Man (1961)," in *For a New Novel*, op. cit., 144.

11. Interview in 1973 with David Hayman, in *Wisconsin Studies in Contemporary Literature* 16.3 (summer 1975): 284.

12. Lecture by Robbe-Grillet at the Carpenter Center, 1976.

13. Alain Robbe-Grillet, "Order and Disorder in Film and Fiction," trans. Bruce Morrissette, *Critical Inquiry* 4.1 (autumn 1977): 14.

14. Jean Ricardou, ed., *Colloque de Cérisy, Alain Robbe-Grillet, 2, Cinéma/Roman* (Paris: Union Générale d'Editions, 1976), 47.

15. Robbe-Grillet, "Order and Disorder in Film and Fiction," 16.

16. Jean Ricardou, ed., *Colloque de Cérisy, Robbe-Grillet, 1, Roman/Cinema*, discussion following Ricardou lecture, "Terrorisme, théorie," 35–36.

17. Franklin Rosemont, ed., *André Breton and the First Principles of Surrealism* (London: Pluto Press, 1978), 108.

18. Statement in a letter to this writer, 7 July 1979.

19. Comments in a lecture by Robbe-Grillet at La Maison Française, New York University, 19 September 1995.

Film Glossary

The following definitions have been selected and quoted from James Monaco, *How to Read a Film* (New York: Oxford University Press, 1977), 395–437. The defined terms concern devices used in creating a film, in addition to critical terms from theories of film language and practice. Many of these devices were used by Robbe-Grillet in his films, certainly the films discussed in this book. Some of the film devices, rhetorical terms, and language theories can be applied to an analysis and understanding of Robbe-Grillet's novels. I am grateful to James Monaco for allowing me to use his terms and definitions.

Accelerated Montage: A sequence edited into progressively shorter shots to create a mood of tension and excitement.

Aerial Shot: A shot taken from a crane, plane, or helicopter. Not necessarily a moving shot.

Aleatory Technique: An artistic technique that utilizes chance conditions and probability. Images and sounds are not planned.

Ambient Light: The natural light surrounding the subject, usually understood to be soft.

Angle of View: The angle subtended by the lens. Wide-angle lenses have broad angles of view; telephoto lenses have very narrow angles of view. Not to be confused with *Camera Angle*.

Arriflex: A lightweight, portable camera introduced in the late 1950s and essential to the *Hand-Held* technique of the *New Wave* and the contemporary style of cinematography that followed in the 1960s. The Arriflex was soon joined by many imitators.

Asynchronous Sound: Sound that does not operate in unison with the image. See *Commentative Sound*.

FILM GLOSSARY

Attraction: Eisenstein's theory of film analyzes the image as a series or connection of attractions, each in a dialectical relationship with the others. Attractions were thus basic elements of film form, and the theory of attractions was a precursor to modern semiotic theory.

Auteur: (1) The prime author of a film. (2) A director with a recognizable style.

Backlighting: The main source of light is behind the subject, silhouetting it, and directed toward the camera. See also *Filler Light, Key Light*.

Bridging Shot: A shot used to cover a jump in time, place, or other discontinuity. Examples are falling calendar pages, railroad wheels, newspaper headlines, seasonal changes.

Cahiers du Cinéma: A seminal film journal founded by André Bazin, Jacques Doniol-Valcroze, and Lo Duca in 1951. Godard, Truffaut, Chabrol, Rohmer, Rivette, and others wrote for it.

Camera Angle: The angle at which the camera is pointed at the subject: low, high, or tilt. Not to be confused with *Angle of View*.

Cinéaste: A filmmaker. More generally, anyone associated in a professional capacity with film.

Cinemagraphic: A general adjective, not in wide use, for the scientific study of film.

Cinematography: Motion-picture photography.

Ciné-Structuralism: The application of *Semiotics* to cinema in an essentially sociological or ethnographic way. The British journal *Screen* is the most important center.

Closeup: (1) Precisely, a shot of the subject's face only. (2) Generally, any close shot.

Codes, Subcodes: In *Semiotics*, the rules and sets of identifiable elements, an understanding of which allows us to interpret a film. Codes are analytic tools constructed after the fact.

Commentative Sound: Sound whose source is outside the reality of the scene being shot. The opposite of the actual sound in the scene. Compare *Asynchronous Sound*.

Content Curve: A term used to denote the amount of time necessary for the average viewer to assimilate most of the meaning of a *Shot*.

Continuity: The script supervisor is in charge of the continuity of a film production, making sure that details in one shot will match details in another, even though the shots may be filmed weeks or months apart. The script supervisor also keeps detailed records of *Takes*.

Cross-cutting: Intermingling the shots of two or more scenes to suggest parallel action.

Cut: In film and television, a switch from one image to another.

Day for Night: The practice of using filters to shoot night scenes during the day.

Découpage: The design of the film, the arrangement of its shots. "Découpage classique" is the French term for the old Hollywood style of seamless narration.

Deep Focus: A technique favored by realists in which objects very near the camera as well as those far away are in focus at the same time.

Depth of Field: The range of distances from the camera at which the subject is acceptably sharp.

Detail Shot: Usually more magnified than a *Closeup*. A shot of a hand, eye, mouth, or subject of similar detail.

Diachronic: In linguistic theory, a phenomenon is diachronic when it consists of or depends upon a change in its state, usually across time. See *Synchronic*.

Diegesis: The **denotative** material of the film narrative, it includes, according to Metz, not only the narration itself but also the fictional space and time dimensions implied by the narrative.

Dissolve: The superimposition of a *Fade Out* over a *Fade In*. Sometimes called a lap dissolve.

Dolly: A set of wheels and a platform upon which the camera can be mounted to give it mobility. Also called "crab dolly."

Dolly Shot: A shot taken from a moving *Dolly*. Almost synonymous with *Tracking Shot*.

Double-System Sound: The technique widely used today in which sound is recorded separately by a lightweight magnetic recorder that is physically separate from the camera although often linked to it for purposes of synchronization.

Dub: (1) To rerecord dialogue in a language other than the original. (2) To record dialogue in a specially equipped studio after the film has been shot.

Ecriture: The French semiological term for that quality of a work of art that is a combination of the artist's personal style and more general social, political, and historical concerns.

Editor: The cutter. The person who determines the narrative structure of a film, in charge of the work of splicing the shots of a film together into final form. See *Fine Cut, Montage*.

FILM GLOSSARY

Emulsion: The thin coating of chemicals, mounted on the base of the filmstock, that reacts to light.

Establishing Shot: Generally, a long shot that shows the audience the general location of the scene that follows, often providing essential information or orienting the viewer.

Extreme Long Shot: A panoramic view of an exterior location photographed from a considerable distance, often as far as a quarter-mile away. See *Establishing Shot*.

Fade In: A punctuation device. The screen is black at the beginning; gradually the image appears, brightening to full strength.

Fade Out: The opposite of *Fade In*. With recent expansion of color filmmaking, some directors now choose to fade from or to a color other than black.

Fast Motion: Also called "accelerated motion." The film is shot at less than twenty-four frames per second so that when it is projected at the normal speed, actions appear to move much faster.

Fill Light, Filler Light: An auxiliary light, usually from the side of the subject, that can soften shadows and illuminate areas not covered by the *Key Light*.

Film Clip: A short section of film taken out of context.

Final Cut: The film as it will be released. The guarantee of final cut assures a filmmaker that the producer will not be able to revise the film after the filmmaker has finished it.

Fine Cut: The film in its final state.

Flashback: A scene or *Sequence* (sometimes an entire film) that is inserted into a scene in "present" time and that deals with the past. The flashback is the past tense of film.

Flash Cutting: Editing the film into shots of very brief duration that succeed each other rapidly.

Flash-Forward: On the model of *Flashback*, scenes or shots of future time; the future tense of film.

Flash Frame: A shot of only a few frames duration—sometimes a single frame—which can just barely be perceived by the audience.

Focus: The sharpness of the image. A range of distances from the camera will be acceptably sharp. See *Deep Focus*.

Focus Pull: To refocus during a take: to change the focus plane.

Follow Shot: A *Tracking Shot* or *Zoom*, which follows the subject as it moves.

Frame: (1) Any single image on the film. (2) The size and shape of the image on the film, or on the screen when projected. (3) The compositional unit of film design.

Freeze Frame: A freeze shot, which is achieved by printing a single frame many times in succession to give the illusion of a still photograph when projected.

Full Shot: A shot of a subject that includes the entire body and not much else.

Gaffer: The chief electrician on the set; in charge of the lights. His assistant is the "best boy."

Ghost Image: A type of double exposure in which one or more preceding frames are printed together with the main frame to give a multiple exposure.

Glass Shot: A type of *Special Effect* in which part of the scene is painted on a clear glass plate mounted in front of the camera.

Grip: The person in charge of props on a set.

Hand-Held: Since the development of lightweight portable cameras, hand-held shots have become more common.

Highlighting: Sometimes pencil-thin beams of light are used to illuminate certain parts of the subject.

Icon: In the Peirce/Wollen semiotics, a sign that represents its object mainly by its similarity to it.

Image: An image is both an optical pattern and a mental experience. (1) A single specific picture. (2) Generally, the visuals of film or media as opposed to sound. (3) A visual *Trope*. (4) By extension, often a nonvisual trope; hence, we speak of aural, poetic, or musical "images."

Index: In the Peirce/Wollen system, a sign that represents its object by virtue of an existential bond. For example, a clock.

Information Theory: Theory that deals with the transmission of messages, considering problems of distribution, transmission, and reception. Christian Metz identifies five separate channels of information: *Images*, graphic representation (words read from the screen), recorded speech, recorded music, and recorded sound effects.

Insert, Insert Shot: A *Detail Shot* that gives specific and relevant information necessary to a complete understanding of the meaning of the scene. Examples: a letter, a tell-tale physical detail.

Iris In, Iris Out: An old technique of punctuation that utilizes a diaphragm in front of the lens that is opened (Iris In) or closed (Iris

Out) to begin or end a scene. The iris can also be used to focus attention on a detail of a scene.

Jump Cut: A cut that occurs within a scene, rather than between scenes, to condense the shot. It can effectively eliminate dead periods.

Key Light: The main light on a subject. Usually placed at a 45° angle to the camera-subject axis.

Language, Language System: English equivalents of the French terms *langage* and *langue*, respectively. Cinema is a language because it is a means of communication, but it is not necessarily a language system because it doesn't follow the rules of written or spoken language.

Lens: An optical lens bends light rays in order to focus them; a magnetic lens bends electron beams so that they can be controlled for the purposes of scanning (a television term).

Library Shot: A *Stock Shot*.

Lip Sync: Synchronization between the movement of the mouth and the words on the soundtrack.

Mask: (1) A shield placed before the camera lens to block off a part of the image. (2) A shield placed behind the projector lens to obtain the correct aspect ratio.

Matte Shot: A matte is a piece of film that is opaque in part of the frame area. When printed together with a normal shot, it masks part of the image of that shot and allows another scene, reverse matted, to be printed in the masked-off area.

Metonymy: In rhetoric, a common figure of speech that is characterized by the substitution of a word or concept closely associated with the object for the object itself (hence, "gun" for "gunman").

Mise en Scène: The term usually used to denote that part of the cinematic process that takes place on the set, as opposed to *Montage*, which takes place afterwards. The direction of actors, placement of cameras, choice of lenses, et cetera.

Montage: (1) Simply, editing. (2) Eisenstein's idea that adjacent shots should relate to each other in such a way that A and B combine to produce another meaning, C, which is not actually recorded on the film. (3) "Dynamic cutting" is a highly stylized editing, often with the purpose of providing a lot of information in a short period of time.

Motif: A recurrent thematic element used in the development of an artistic work.

Multiple Image: A number of images printed beside each other within the same frame, often showing different camera angles of the same action or separate actions. Also called *Split Screen*.

Music Track: One of three basic tracks, together with dialogue and effects, that are mixed together to form the final soundtrack.

Narration: Spoken description or analysis of action.

Narrative Story: the linear, chronological structure of a story.

Negative Image: An image in which blacks are white and vice versa.

New Wave, Nouvelle Vague: (1) Godard, Truffaut, Chabrol, Rohmer, Rivette, and so on. (2) The term is also used more loosely to refer to either all the young French filmmakers of the 1960s or any new group of filmmakers.

Optical: An operation accomplished in the laboratory rather than on the *Set* or in the cutting room. Examples: *Dissolves, Freeze Frames, Ghost Images,* and *Matte Shots, Wipes.*

Overlap Sound: A cut in which the cut in the soundtrack is not synchronous with the cut in the image.

Over-the-Shoulder Shot: A shot commonly used in dialogue scenes in which the speaker is seen from the perspective of a person standing just behind and a little to one side of the listener, so that parts of the head and shoulder of the listener, as well as the head of the speaker, are in the frame.

Pan: Movement of the camera from left to right or right to left around the imaginary vertical axis that runs through the camera.

Paradigm: In *Semiology,* a unit of potential, as opposed to actual, relationship: "What elements or statements go with what"; see *Syntagma.*

Point-of-View Shot: A shot that shows the scene from the point of view of a character. Often abbreviated as "pov."

Process Shot: *Matte Shots, Opticals, Rear Projection,* and the like.

Pull-Back Shot: A *Tracking Shot* or *Zoom* that moves back from the subject to reveal the context of the scene.

Rack Focusing: A technique that uses shallow focus (shallow *Depth of Field*) to direct the attention of the viewer forcibly from one subject to another.

Reaction Shot: A shot that cuts away from the main scene or speaker in order to show a character's reaction to it.

Rear Projection: A process in which a background scene is projected onto a translucent screen behind the actors so it appears the actors are in that location. Superseded at present by front projection and *Matte Shot* techniques, both more effective systems.

Reverse Angle: (1) A *Shot* from the opposite side of a subject. (2) In a dialogue scene, a shot of the second participant.

Reverse Motion: The film is run through the camera backwards so that, when it is later run through the projector in the normal manner, the illusion will be created that time is running backwards.

Room Sound, Room Noise, Room Tone: (1) The particular quality of sound in a certain location, mainly a matter of reverberation and echoes. (2) The basic, underlying sound present in a location, such as clocks, traffic, activity. Room sound is often recorded "wild" and later mixed with dialogue and effects.

Scenario: (1) An outline for a *Screenplay*. (2) A complete screenplay.

Screenplay: The script of a film or television show, usually but not necessarily including rough descriptions of camera movements as well as dialogue.

Semiology, Semiotics: Theory of criticism pioneered by Roland Barthes in literature and Christian Metz, Umberto Eco, and Peter Wollen in film. It uses the theories of modern linguistics, especially Ferdinand de Saussure's concept of signification.

Sequence: A basic unit of film construction consisting of one or more scenes that form a natural unit.

Set: The location of a scene, usually artificially constructed on a sound stage.

Set-Up: A camera and lighting position. When large, unwieldy cameras and lights are used, the number of different set-ups required can become an important economic factor.

Shot: A single piece of film, however long or short, without cuts, exposed continuously. A film may be composed of more than a thousand shots, or it may seem to be a single shot.

Slow Motion: The camera is overcranked so that the film runs through faster than the normal twenty-four frames per second. When the film is projected at the normal rate, the action takes more time than in reality. See *Fast Motion*.

Soft Focus: Filters, vaseline, or specially constructed lenses soften the delineation of lines and points, usually to create a romantic effect.

Sound: See *Asynchronous, Commentative, Overlap,* and *Synchronous*.

Sound Effects: All those created sounds that are not dialogue or music.

Special Effects: A broad term for a wide range of devices and processes, including some kinds of work performed by stunt men.

Split Screen: Two or more separate images within the frame that do not overlap. Accomplished on an optical printer (for film).

Stock Shot: (1) A library shot, which is literally borrowed from a collection such as of World War II shots, jet planes in flight, or *Establishing Shots* of New York City. (2) Any unimaginative or common shot that looks as if it might as well have been a library shot.

Subjective Camera: A style that allows the viewer to observe events from the point of view of either a character or the persona of the author. See *Point-of-View Shot*.

Swish Pan: Also called flick pan, zip pan, whip pan. A *Pan* in which the intervening scene moves past too quickly to be observed.

Symbol: (1) In the Peirce/Wollen system, a sign that demands neither resemblance to its object nor any existential bond with it but operates by pure convention. (2) More generally, something that represents something else by resemblance, association, or convention.

Synchronic: In *Semiological* theory, a phenomenon is synchronic when all its elements belong to the same moment in time and do not depend on a change of state across time.

Syntagma: A *Semiological* term. A unit of actual rather than potential relationship. Syntagmatic relationships exist between the present elements of a shot or a statement in film. The syntagma describes what follows what, rather than what goes with what.

Tilt Shot: The camera tilts up or down, rotating around the axis that runs from left to right through the camera head. See *Pan*.

Tracking Shot: Generally, any shot in which the camera moves from one point to another sideways, in, or out. The camera can be mounted on a set of wheels that move on tracks or on a rubber-tired *Dolly*, or it can be *Hand-Held*. Also called "traveling shot."

Trope: Any artistic device, such as a figure of speech or a symbol; a connotative twist or turn in meaning. As a comprehensive art, film can avail itself of the tropes of many other arts.

Vignette: A *Masking* device, often with soft edges... See also *Iris In, Iris Out*.

Voice-Over: The narrator's voice when the narrator is not seen. See *Commentative Sound*.

Wipe: An optical effect in which an image appears to "wipe off" the preceding image. Very common in the 1930s, less so today.

Zoom: A shot using a lens whose focal length is adjusted during the shot. The focal lengths of which the lens is capable range from wide angle to telephoto. Zooms are sometimes used in place of *Tracking Shots*, but the differences between the two are significant.

Selected Bibliography

Theories of Representation and Surrealism

Alquié, Ferdinand. *The Philosophy of Surrealism*. Translated by B. Waldrop. Ann Arbor: The University of Michigan Press, 1969.

Arnheim, Rudolph. *Art and Visual Perception*. Berkeley: University of California Press, 1974.

Auerbach, Erich. *Mimesis: The Representation of Reality in Western Literature*. Translated by Willard Trask. Princeton: Princeton University Press, 1968.

Block, Haskell. *Naturalistic Triptych: The Fictive and the Real in Zola, Mann, and Dreiser*. New York: Random House, 1970.

Fischer, Ernest. *The Necessity of Art: A Marxist Approach*. Translated by Anna Bostock. Harmondsworth: Penguin Books, 1963.

Flaubert, Gustave. *Letters*. Edited by Richard Rumbold and translated by J. M. Cohen. London: George Weidenfelt and Nicholson Ltd., 1950.

Fowlie, Wallace. *Age of Surrealism*. Bloomington: Indiana University Press, 1972.

Ghiselin, Michael T. "Poetic Biology—a Defense and Manifesto." *New Literary History* 7.3 (spring 1973): 493–503.

Greenblatt, Stephen J., ed. *Allegory and Representation*. Selected papers from the English Institute, 1979–80. Baltimore and London: Johns Hopkins University Press, 1981.

———. *Learning to Curse*. New York: Routledge, 1990.

Hyde, William J. "George Eliot and the Climate of Realism." *PMLA* 72.1 (March 1957): 147–64.

Kadarskay, Arpad, ed. *The Lukacs Reader*. Oxford, U.K., and Cambridge, USA: Blackwell, 1995.

Kermode, Frank. *The Genesis of Secrecy: On the Interpretation of Narrative*. The Charles Eliot Norton Lectures. Cambridge, USA, and London, England: Harvard University Press, 1979.

———. *The Sense of an Ending: Studies in the Theory of Fiction*. London: Oxford University Press, 1967.

Lessing, Gotthold Ephraim. *Laocoön: An Essay on the Limits of Painting and Poetry.* Translated by Edward Allen McCormick. Baltimore and London: The Johns Hopkins University Press, 1984. Originally published 1766.

Lippard, Lucy, ed. *Surrealists on Art.* Englewood Cliffs, N.J.: Prentice-Hall Inc., 1970.

Matthews, J. W. *Surrealism and the Novel.* Ann Arbor: University of Michigan Press, 1969.

Osborne, Harold. *Aesthetics and Art Theory.* New York: E. P. Dutton, 1970.

——, ed. *Aesthetics in the Modern World.* New York: Weybright and Talley, 1968.

Read, Herbert, ed. *Surrealism.* New York: Praeger Publishers, 1971.

Rosemont, Franklin, ed. *André Breton and the First Principles of Surrealism.* London: Pluto Press, 1978.

Rossi, Vino. *André Gide: The Evolution of an Aesthetic.* New Brunswick, N.J.: Rutgers University Press, 1967.

Scholes, Robert, ed. *Approaches to the Novel: Material for a Poetics.* San Francisco: Chandler Publishing Co., 1966.

Siegel, Ronald. "Hallucinations." In *The Mind's Eye: Readings from Scientific American*, 109–16. New York: W. H. Freeman and Company, 1976–86.

Todorov, Tzvetan. *The Fantastic: A Structural Approach to a Literary Genre.* Translated by Richard Howard. Ithaca, N.Y.: Cornell University Press, 1975.

——. *Symbolism and Interpretation.* Translated by Catherine Porter. Ithaca, N.Y.: Cornell University Press, 1982.

Weinstein, Arnold L. *Vision and Response in Modern Fiction.* Ithaca, N.Y.: Cornell University Press, 1974.

Wheelwright, Philip. *Metaphor and Reality.* Bloomington: Indiana University Press, 1964.

Wollheim, Richard. "Art and Illusion." In *Aesthetics in the Modern World*, edited by Harold Osborne. New York: Weybright and Talley, 1968.

Theories of Phenomenology, Postmodernism, Semiology, and Art

Bachelard, Gaston. *The Poetics of Space.* Translated by Maria Jolas. Boston: Beacon Press, 1969.

Barthes, Roland. *Critical Essays.* Translated by Richard Miller. New York: Hill and Wang, 1974.

——. *Elements of Semiology.* Translated by Annette Laver and Colin Smith. New York: Hill and Wang, 1964.

——. *S/Z: An Essay.* Translated by Richard Miller. New York: Hill and Wang, 1974. Originally published by Les Editions du Seuil, Paris, 1970.

———. *Image-Music-Text. Essays Selected and Translated by Stephen Heath*. New York: Hill and Wang, 1977.
Carr, David, ed. *Explorations in Phenomenology*. The Hague: Martinus Nijhoff, 1973.
Chapman, Raymond, ed. *Linguistics and Literature: An Introduction to Literary Stylistics*. Totowa, N.J.: Littlefield, Adams, and Co., 1973.
Chatman, Seymour. *Selected Papers from the English Institute: Approaches to Poetics*. New York: Columbia University Press, 1973.
———. *Literary Style: A Symposium*. London: Oxford University Press, 1971.
Derrida, Jacques. *Speech and Phenomena and Other Essays on Husserl's Theory of Signs*. Evanston, Ill.: Northwestern University Press, 1973.
———. *Writing and Difference*. Translated by Alan Bass. Chicago: The University of Chicago Press, 1978.
de Saussure, Ferdinand. *Course in General Linguistics*. Edited by Charles Bally and Albert Schehaye. Translated by Wade Baskin. New York: McGraw Hill, 1966.
Eco, Umberto. *Six Walks in the Fictional Woods*. The Charles Eliot Norton Lectures. Cambridge, USA, and London, England: Harvard University Press, 1994.
Farber, Marvin. *Phenomenology and Existence: Toward a Philosophy within Nature*. New York: Harper and Row, 1967.
y Gasset, Jose Ortega. *Phenomenology and Art*. Translated by Philip Silver. New York: W. W. Norton, 1975.
Gurwitsch, Aron. "The Phenomenology of Perception." In *An Invitation to Phenomenology*, edited by James M. Edie, 18–28. Chicago: Quadrangle Books, 1965.
Hawkes, Terence. *Structuralism and Semiotics*. Berkeley and Los Angeles: University of California Press, 1977.
Heidegger, Martin. *Basic Writings*. New York: Harper and Row, 1977.
———. *The Essence of Reasons*. A bilingual edition. Translated by Terence Malick. Studies in Phenomenology and Existential Philosophy Series. Evanston, Ill.: Northwestern University Press, 1969.
Hoesterey, Ingeborg, ed. *Zeitgeist in Babel: The Postmodernist Controversy*. Bloomington and Indianapolis: Indiana University Press, 1991.
Husserl, Edmund [1913]. *Ideas: General Introduction to Pure Phenomenology*. Translated by R. Boyce Gibson. London: Collier Macmillan Publishers, 1962.
———. *The Idea of Phenomenology, Based on Lectures Given in 1907*. Translated by W. Alson and G. Nahnikian. The Hague: Martinus Nijhoff, 1973.
Iser, Wolfgang. *The Act of Reading: A Theory of Aesthetic Response*. Baltimore and London: The Johns Hopkins University Press. 1978.
———. *The Implied Reader. Patterns of Communication in Prose Fiction from Bunyan to Beckett*. Baltimore and London: The Johns Hopkins University Press, 1974.
———. "The reading process: a phenomenological approach." In *Modern Criticism and Theory*, edited by David Lodge, 211–28. London and New York: Longman, 1988.

Jakobson, Roman. *Six Lectures on Sound and Meaning*. Translated by John Mepham. Cambridge, USA, and London, England: MIT Press, 1978.

Jameson, Frederic. *Postmodernism or The Cultural Logic of Late Capitalism*. Durham: Duke University Press, 1991.

Kaelin, Eugene. "The Visibility of Things Seen." In *An Invitation to Phenomenology*, edited by James M. Edie, 37–42. Chicago: Quadrangle Books, 1965.

Langer, Susanne K. "On Significance in Music." In *Philosophy in a New Key*, 206–7. New York: New American Library, 1951.

"The Language of Images," *Critical Inquiry* 6.3 (spring 1980).

Lentricchia, Frank. *After the New Criticism*. Chicago: University of Chicago Press, 1980.

Lodge, David, ed. *Modern Criticism and Theory, A Reader*. London and New York: Longman, 1988.

Lukács, Georg. "On the Phenomenology of the Creative Process." In *The Philosophical Forum*. Department of Philosophy, Boston University. Spring–summer 1972: 321.

Magliola, Robert R. *Phenomenology and Literature: An Introduction*. Indiana: Purdue University Press; 1977.

Mallin, Samuel B. *Merleau-Ponty's Philosophy*. New Haven and London: Yale University Press, 1979.

Melville, Stephen. *Philosophy beside Itself: On Deconstruction and Modernism*. Minneapolis: University of Minnesota Press, 1986.

Merleau-Ponty, Maurice. *Phenomenology of Perception*. Translated by Colin Smith. New York: Humanities Press, 1962.

———. *The Primacy of Perception and Other Essays*. Edited and translated by James M. Edie. Evanston, Ill.: Northwestern University Press, 1964.

———. *Sense and Non-Sense*. Translated by Herbert I. Dreyfus and Patricia A. Dreyfus. Evanston, Illinois: Northwestern University Press, 1964.

———. *Humanism and Terror: An Essay on the Communist Problem*. Translated by John O'Neill. Boston: Beacon Press, 1969.

Moxey, Keith. *The Practice of Theory: Poststructuralism, Cultural Politics, and Art History*. Ithaca, N.Y.: Cornell University Press, 1994.

Molina, Fernando. "The Husserlian Ideal of a Pure Phenomenology." In *An Invitation to Phenomenology*, edited and translated by James M. Edie, 162–67. Chicago: Quadrangle Books., 1965.

Morris, Charles. *Signification and Significance: A Study of the Relation of Signs and Values*. Cambridge, Mass.: MIT Press, 1964.

O'Neill, John. *Perception, Expression and History: The Phenomenology of Maurice Merleau-Ponty*. Evanston, Ill.: Northwestern University Press, 1970.

Perc, Jerzy. *Studies in Functional Logical Semiotics of Natural Language*. The Hague: Mouton, 1971.

Pettit, Philip. *The Concept of Structuralism: a Critical Analysis*. Berkeley and Los Angeles: University of California Press, 1977.

Ramat, Paolo. "Semiotics and Linguistics." *Versus* 10.1 (April 1975): 4.

Rastier, François. *Essais de Semiotique Discursive*. Paris: Maison Mame, 1973.

Sebeok, Thomas, ed. *Style in Language: Conference on Style*. Cambridge, Mass.: MIT Press, 1960.

Szanto, George. *Narrative Consciousness*. Austin: University of Texas Press, 1972.

Thévenaz, Pierre. *What Is Phenomenology? And Other Essays*. Edited and with an introduction by James M. Edie; translated by Edie, Courtney, Brockelman. Chicago: Quadrangle Books, 1962.

Torczyner, Harry. *Magritte, Ideas, and Images*. Translated by Richard Miller. New York: Harry N. Abrams. Inc., 1977.

van Peursen, Cornelis A. *Phenomenology and Reality*. Pittsburgh: Duquesne University Press, 1972.

Wellek, René. "The Parallelism between Literature and Art." *English Institute Annual* 1941.

The French New Novel and Theories of Narrative

Brée, Germaine and Margaret Guiton. *An Age of Fiction: The French Novel from Gide to Camus*. New Brunswick, N.J.: Rutgers University Press, 1957.

Cruikshank, John, ed. *The Novelist as Philosopher: Studies in French Fiction 1935–1960*. London: Oxford University Press, 1962.

Dilonardo Troiano, Maureen. *New Physics and the Modern French Novel: An Investigation of Interdisciplinary Discourse*. New York: Peter Lang, 1994.

Goldmann, Lucien. "Nouveau Roman et réalité." In *Pour une sociologie du roman*. Paris: Gallimard, 1964.

Heath, Stephen. *The Nouveau Roman: A Study in the Practice of Writing*. London: Elek, 1977.

Jefferson, Ann. *The Nouveau Roman and the Poetics of Fiction*. Cambridge, London, New York, New Rochelle, Melbourne, and Sydney: Cambridge University Press, 1980.

Levi, Albert William. "Literature, Philosophy, and the Imagination." *The Journal of Aesthetic Education* 5.22 (winter 1988): 9–20.

Le Sage, Laurent. *The French New Novel*. State College: Pennsylvania State University Press, 1962.

Mauriac, Claude. *The New Literature*. Translated by Samuel I. Stone. New York: G. Braziller, 1959.

Nelson, Roy Jay. *Causality and Narrative in French Fiction from Zola to Robbe-Grillet*. Columbus: Ohio State University Press, 1990.

Novel: A Forum on Fiction. "Why the Novel Matters: A Postmodern Perplex." Special issue. 21 (April 1988).

Peyre, Henri. *French Novelists of Today*. New York: Oxford University Press, 1967.

Ricardou, Jean and Françoise van Rossum-Guyon, eds. *Nouveau Roman: hièr, aujourd'hui*. Paris: Union Générale d'Editions, 1972.

———. "Page, film, récit." *Cahiers du Cinéma* 185 (December 1966): 71–74.

Sarraute, Nathalie. *The Age of Suspicion*. New York: George Braziller, 1963.

Simon, Claude. "Reflections on the Novel." *The Review of Contemporary Fiction* 5.1 (spring 1985): 14–23.

Stoltzfus, Ben. F. *Alain Robbe-Grillet and the New French Novel*. Carbondale: Southern Illinois Press, 1964.

———. *Alain Robbe-Grillet: The Body of the Text*. Cranbury, N.J.: Associated University Presses, 1985.

Sturrock, John. *The French New Novel*. London: Oxford University Press, 1969.

Sypher, Wylie. *Loss of the Self in Modern Literature and Art*. New York: Random House, 1962.

General Literature on Alain Robbe-Grillet

Alter, Jean. *La Vision du monde d'Alain Robbe-Grillet: structures et significations*. Geneva: Libraire Droz, 1966.

———. "Alain Robbe-Grillet and the 'Cinematographic Style.'" *Modern Language Journal* 48.6 (October 1964): 363–66.

Barthes, Roland. "Objective Literature: Alain Robbe-Grillet." Introductory essay in *Two Novels* by Robbe-Grillet, translated by Richard Howard. New York: Grove Press, 1965.

Bernal, Olga. *Alain Robbe-Grillet: le roman de l'absence*. Paris: Gallimard, 1964. Also *Dissertation Abstracts* 25.6 (December 1964): 3564–65.

Bogue, Ronald L. "Meaning and Ideology in Robbe-Grillet's Topologie d'une cité fantôme." Modern Language Studies 14.1 (winter 1984): 33–46.

Chapsal, Madeleine. "Books: Who Is Robbe-Grillet?" *The Reporter*, 14 July 1966, pp. 54–57.

Chery, Christian. "Alain Robbe-Grillet ou le nouveau réalisme." *Pensée Française* 16.12 (November 1957): 17–19.

Cladwell, R. C. "The Robbe-Grillet Game: Mankind's Ludic Condition in the 20th Century." *French Review* 5.65 (March 1992): 547–56.

Durozoi, Gerard. *Les Gommes: Robbe-Grillet; Analyse, Critique*. Paris: Hatier, 1973.

Fragola, Anthony N. and Roch C. Smith. *The Erotic Dream Machine: Interviews with Alain Robbe-Grillet on His Films*. Carbondale: Southern Illinois University Press, 1992.

SELECTED BIBLIOGRAPHY

Frazier, Dale Watson. *Alain Robbe-Grillet: An Annotated Bibliography of Critical Studies, 1953–1972*. The Scarecrow Author Bibliographies, no. 13. Metuchen, N.J.: The Scarecrow Press, Inc., 1973.

Freeman, Judi. *Mark Tansey Catalogue*. Los Angeles County Museum of Art. San Francisco: Chronicle Books, 1993.

Gardies, André, ed. "Alain Robbe-Grillet: Textes et Documents." In *Cinéma d'aujourd'hui 70*. Paris: Editions Seghers, 1972.

Harger-Grinling, Virginia and Tony Chadwick, eds. *Robbe-Grillet and the Fantastic: A Collection of Essays*. Westport, Conn.: Greenwood Press, 1994.

Hellerstein, Marjorie H. "One Autobiographer's Reality: Robbe-Grillet." Edited by M. Kronegger. In *Analecta Husserliana*, 32: 39–48. Netherlands: Kluwer Academic Publishers, 1990.

Kafalenos, Emma. "Image and Narrativity: Robbe-Grillet's La Belle Captive Containing more than Seventy-five of Magritte's Paintings." *Visible Language* 23 (autumn 1989): 375–92.

Kochbar-Lindgren, Gray. "The Cocked Eye: Robbe-Grillet, Lacan, and the Desire to See it All." *American Imago* 49.4 (winter 1992): 467.

Leenhardt, Jacques. *Lecture Politique du Roman: La Jalousie d'Alain Robbe-Grillet*. Paris: Les Editions du Minuit, 1973.

———. "Pages d'écriture sur fond des ruines." *Obliques* 16–17 (1978): 133–40.

Mauriac, Claude. "Alain Robbe-Grillet." Translated by Samuel I. Stone. In *The New Literature*. New York: G. Braziller, 1959.

Miesch, Jean. *Robbe-Grillet*. Paris: Editions Universitaires, 1965.

Micciollo, Henri. *"La Jalousie" d'Alain Robbe-Grillet*. Paris: Librairie Hachette, 1972.

Morrissette, Bruce. *Intertextual Assemblage in Robbe-Grillet from Topology to the Golden Triangle*. Fredericton, N.B., Canada: York Press, 1979.

———. *The Novels of Robbe-Grillet*. Ithaca: Cornell University Press, 1975. First published in Paris: Les Editions de Minuit, 1963.

———. "Robbe-Grillet as a Critic of Samuel Becket." In *Samuel Becket Now: Critical Approaches to His Novels, Poetry, and Plays*, edited by Melvin J. Friedman. Chicago: University of Chicago Pres, 1970.

O'Donnell, Thomas D. "Thematic Generation in Robbe-Grillet's *Projet pour une révolution à New York*." In *Twentieth-Century French Fiction: Essays for Germaine Brée*. New Brunswick, N.J.: Rutgers University Press, 1975.

Ortquist, Leslie. "Magritte's Captivity in Robbe-Grillet's *La Belle Captive*: The Subjugation of the Image by the Work." *Visible Language* 5.23 (spring–summer 1990): 238–53.

Ramsey, Raylene. *Robbe-Grillet and Modernity: Science, Sexuality, and Subversion*. Gainsville, etc.: University Press of Florida, 1993.

———. *The French New Autobiographies: Sarraute, Duras, and Robbe-Grillet*. Gainsville, etc.: University Press of Florida. 1996.

Ricardou, Jean, ed. *Colloque de Cérisy. Robbe-Grillet: 1. Roman/Cinéma.* Union Genérale d'Editions, 1976.

———. *Colloque de Cérisy. Robbe-Grillet: 2. Cinéma/Roman.* Union Genérale d'Editions, 1976.

Suleiman, Susan. "Reading Robbe-Grillet: Sadism and Text in Projet pour une révolution à New York." *Romanic Review* 68 (January 1977): 43–62.

van Wert, William F. *The Film Career of Alain Robbe-Grillet.* Pleasantville, N.Y.: Redgrave Publishing Co., 1977.

Vidal, Jean-Pierre. "Remise au jour d'un polyptique insoupçonne de Magritte: *La Belle Captive.*" In *Obliques*, edited by François Jost, 213–24. Paris: Editions Broderie, 1978.

Film Language and Analysis

Andrew, J. Dudley. *The Major Film Theories.* London: Oxford University Press, 1976.

Armes, Roy. *French Cinema since 1946.* Vol. 2: *The Personal Style.* South Brunswick, N.J.: A. S. Barnes, 1970.

Bazin, André. *What is Cinema?* Vol. 2. Essays selected and translated by Hugh Gray. Berkeley and Los Angeles: University of California Press, 1971.

Burch, Noël. *Theory of Film Practice.* Translated by Helen R. Lane. New York: Praeger Publishers, Inc., 1973. Originally published in Paris: Editions Gallimard, 1969.

Doniol-Valcroze, Jacques. "Istanbul nous appartient." *Cahiers du cinéma* 34.38 (May 1963): 54–57.

Eichenbaum, Boris. "Problems of Film Stylistics." Translated by T. Aman. *Screen* 40.3 (autumn 1974): 7–32.

Eisenstein, Sergei. *Film Essays and a Lecture.* Edited by Jey Leyda. New York: Praeger Publishers, Inc., 1970.

Gardies, André. *Le Cinéma d'Alain Robbe-Grillet: essai semiocritique.* Paris: Editions Albatros, 1983.

———, ed. "Alain Robbe-Grillet." In *Cinéma d'aujourd'hui 70.* Paris: Editions Seghers, 1972.

Geduld, Harry. *Filmmakers on Filmmaking.* Bloomington: Indiana University Press, 1967.

———. *Authors on Film.* Bloomington: Indiana University Press, 1972.

Meades, Jonathan. "Alain Robbe-Grillet: The Immortal One." *Books and Bookmen* 17.4 (January 1972): 54–56.

Metz, Christian. *Film Language: A Semiotics of the Cinema.* Translated by Michael Taylor. New York: Oxford University Press, 1974.

———. "Trucage and the Film." *Critical Inquiry* 3.4 (summer 1977): 657–75.
Mitry, Jean, ed. "Le Cinéma des origines." *Cinéma d'aujourd'hui* 9 (automne 1976).
Monaco, James. *How to Read a Film*. New York: Oxford University Press, 1977.
Morrissette, Bruce. "Last Year at Istanbul." *Film Quarterly* 20.2 (winter 1966): 38–42.
———. "Robbe-Grillet at the University of Chicago." *French Review* 50.1 (October 1976): 655–57.
Obliques 16–17 (September 1978). Robbe-Grillet issue edited by François Jost.
Pudovkin, V. I. *Film Technique and Film Acting*. Translated by Ivor Montague. New York: Bonanza Books, 1949.
Sollers, Phillippe. "Le Rève en pleine jour." *La Nouvelle Revue Française* 11 (May 1963): 904–11.
Sosenke, Alexander. "Cinema Space." In *Explorations in Phenomenology*, edited by David Carr and Edward S. Casey, 398–409. The Hague: Martinus Nijhoff, 1973.
Sturdza, Paltin. "The Rebirth Archetype in Robbe-Grillet's L'Immortelle." *French Review* 48.6 (May 1975): 990–95.
Towarnicki, Frederic de. "L'Homme qui ment: Procès verbal." *Cinéma* 67.121 (1967): 57–64.
Wollen, Peter. *Signs and Meaning in the Cinema*. Bloomington: Indiana University Press, 1969.

Interrelationships of Novel and Film

Armes, Roy. "The Reality of Imagination." In *The Ambiguous Image: Narrative Style in Modern European Cinema*, 131–40. Bloomington: Indiana University Press, 1976.
Audry, C. "Robbe-Grillet." *La Revue des Lettres Modernes (Cinéma et Roman)* 5.36–38 (summer 1966).
Bluestone, George. *Novels into Film*. Baltimore: The Johns Hopkins University Press, 1957.
Decaudin, Michel. "Roman et Cinéma." *Revue des Sciences Humaines* n.s. 104 (October-December 1961): 623–28.
Dreyfus, Dina. "Cinéma et Roman." *La Revue d'Esthetique* 15.1 (January-March 1966): 75–84.
Eichenbaum, Boris. "Literature and Cinema," translated by T. E. Aman. *Twentieth-Century Studies* 7–8 (December 1972): 122–27.
Gardies, André. "L'Enjue du Texte Pluriel du Recit Mis à Mal." In *Cahiers du 20e siècle: cinéma et littérature*, 117–43. Paris: Editions Klincksieck, 1978.

———. "Vers un mode de rapport nouveau avec le spectator: le ludique." In *Cahiers du 20ieme siècle: cinéma et littérature*, 93–102. Paris: Editions Klincksieck, 1978.

Gollub, Judith Podselver. "Nouveau Roman et nouveau cinéma." *Dissertation Abstracts* 26.11 (May 1966): 6712–13.

Harrington, John. *Film and/as Literature*. Englewood Cliffs, N.J.: Prentice Hall, Inc., 1977.

Marcus, Fred. H. *Film and Literature: Contrasts in Media*. Scranton, London, Toronto: Chandler Publishing Co., 1971.

Morrissette, Bruce. "Post-Modern Generative Fiction: Novel and Film." *Critical Inquiry* 2.2 (winter 1975): 252–62.

Resnais, Alain and Alain Robbe-Grillet. *Evolution d'une écriture*, Paris: Lettres Modernes, Menard, 1974. Etudes Cinématographiques.

Richardson, Robert. "Film and Modern Fiction." In *Literature and Film*, 79–90. Bloomington: Indiana University Press, 1969.

Ropars-Wuilleumier, Marie-Claire. *De la Littérature au cinema*. Paris: Armand Colin, 1970.

Rybalka, Michel. "Théorie? Anti-Théorie? Robbe-Grillet à Cérisy." *Le Monde*, No. 9484, 18 July 1975, p. 12.

Wagner, Geoffrey. *The Novel and the Cinema*. Cranbury, N.J.: Associated University Presses, Inc., 1975.

Works by Alain Robbe-Grillet

———. *Les Gommes*. Paris: Les Editions de Minuit, 1953. Translated by Richard Howard as *The Erasers*. New York: Grove Press, 1962.

———. *Le Voyeur*. Paris: Les Editions de Minuit, 1955. Translated by Richard Howard as *The Voyeur*. New York: Grove Press, 1958.

———. *La Jalousie*. Paris: Les Editions de Minuit, 1957. Translated by Richard Howard as *Jealousy*. New York: Grove Press, 1959.

———. *Dans le labyrinthe*. Paris: Les Editions de Minuit, 1959. Translated by Richard Howard as *In the Labyrinth*. New York: Grove Press, 1960.

———. *L'Année dernière à Marienbad*. Paris: Les Editions de Minuit, 1961. Translated by Richard Howard as *Last Year at Marienbad*. New York: Grove Press, 1962.

———. *Instantanés*. Paris: Les Editions de Minuit, 1962. Translated by Barbara Wright as *Snapshots*. London: Calder and Boyars, 1965.

———. *Pour un nouveau roman*. Paris: Gallimard, 1963. Translated by Richard Howard as *For a New Novel: Essays on Fiction*. New York: Grove Press, 1965.

———. *L'Immortelle*. Ciné-roman. Paris: Les Editions de Minuit, 1963. Translated by A. M. Sheridan Smith as *The Immortal One*. London: Calder and Boyars, 1971.

———. *La Maison de rendezvous*. Paris: Les Editions de Minuit, 1965. Translated by Richard Howard as *The House of Assignation*. New York: Grove Press Inc., 1966.

———. *Trans-Europ-Express*. Unpublished film directed by Robbe-Grillet, who plays a part in it. 1966.

———. *Projet pour une revolution à New York*. Paris: Les Editions de Minuit, 1970. Translated by Richard Howard as *Project for a Revolution in New York*. New York: Grove Press, 1972.

———. *Les Demoiselles*. Paris: Les Editions de Minuit, 1973. Photographs by David Hamilton. Translated by Martha Egan as *Sisters*. New York: Morrow, 1973.

———. *Glissements progressifs du plaisir*. Ciné-roman and film directed by the author. Paris: Les Editions de Minuit, 1974. Not translated.

———. *Construction d'un temple en ruines a la Déese Vanade*. Text by Robbe-Grillet, etchings by Paul Delvaux. Paris: Editions le Bateau-Lavoir, 1975.

———. *La Belle Captive*. Lausanne and Paris: La Bibliothèque des Arts, 1975. Paintings by René Magritte, translated and with an essay by Ben Stoltzfus. Berkeley: University of California Press, 1995.

———. *Topologie d'une cité fantôme*. Paris: Les Editions de Minuit, 1976. Translated by by J. A. Underwood as *Topology of a Phantom City*. New York: Grove Press, 1977.

———. *Souvenirs du triangle d'or*. Paris Les Editions de Minuit, 1978.

———. *Un Régicide*. Paris: Les Editions de Minuit, 1978.

———. *Le Rendez-vous*. Grammatical exercises by Yvone Lenard. New York: Holt, Rinehart, and Winston, 1981.

———. *Djinn*. Paris: Les Editions de Minuit, 1981. Translated by Yvone Lenard and Walter Wells as *Djinn*. New York: Grove Press Inc., 1982.

———. *Le Miroir qui revient*. Paris: Les Editions de Minuit, 1984. Translated by Jo Levy as *Ghosts in the Mirror*. New York: Grove Weidenfeld, 1988.

———. *Angélique ou l'enchantement*. Paris: Les Editions de Minuit, 1988.

———. *Les Derniers Jours de Corinthe*. Paris: Les Editions de Minuit, 1994.

——— and René Magritte. *La Belle Captive*. Lausanne-Paris: La Bibliothèque des Arts, 1975. Illustrations courtesy of Mme. Georgette Magritte, Bruxelles.

The films *L'Homme qui ment* (The man who lies), 1968; *Eden et après* (Eden and after), 1971; and *Le Jeu avec le feu* (Playing with fire), 1975, have been shown in France and the United States but have no published film-novels or film scripts. His most recent film (1995) is *The Blue Villa* (Un Bruit qui rend fou), directed with Dimitri de Clercq.

Interviews with Alain Robbe-Grillet

Bray, Barbara. "Robbe-Grillet Talks to Barbara Bray." *The Observer*, 942.8, 18 November 1962, p. 23.

Cappele, Anne. "Robbe-Grillet: mon dernier film." *La Quinzain Littéraire*, 48, 1–15 April 1968, pp. 24–25.

Dumont, Lillian and Sandra Silverberg. "An Interview with Alain Robbe-Grillet." *Filmmaker's Newsletter* 9 (9 July 1976).

———. "An Interview with Alain Robbe-Grillet." *French Review* 50.4 (March 1977): 653–55.

Hayman, David. "An Interview with Alain Robbe-Grillet." *Contemporary Literature* 16.3 (summer 1975): 273–85.

Langston, Beverly. "An Interview with Alain Robbe-Grillet." *Yale French Studies* 57 (1979): 228–37.

Robbe-Grillet, Alain. "The French New Novel." Translated by Anna Otten. *Antioch Review* 47 (summer 1987): 200–202.

Schwartz, Paul "Anti-humanism in Art: Interview with Paul Schwartz." *Studio* 175 (April 1968): 168–69.

Weil, Jenny. "A Talk with Alain Robbe-Grillet." *The New Leader* 55.15 (24 July 1972): 12–15.

Articles and Lectures by Robbe-Grillet

———. "Comment mesurer l'inventeur de mesures?" *L'Express*, 627 (June 1963): 44–45.

———. "Brèves Reflexions sur le fait de decrire une scène de cinéma. Antinomie du film et du roman." *La Revue d'Esthetique* 20 (1966): 131–38.

———. "L'Homme qui ment." *La Quinzaine Littéraire* 48 (1968): n.p.

———. "Lettre à Cinema 70." *Cinema 70* 149 (September-October 1970): 100–102.

———. "Sur le choix des generateurs," *Nouveau Roman: hièr, aujourd'hui, Colloque de Cérisy: II. Pratique*, ed. Jean Ricardou. Paris: Union Générale d'Editions, 1972, 157–62.

———. Lecture and presentation of *L'homme qui ment*, at Carpenter Center, Harvard University, April 1976.

———. "Order and Disorder in Film and Fiction." *Critical Inquiry* 4.1 (autumn 1977): 1–20.

———. "A Graveyard of Identities and Uniforms." *Mark Tansey Exhibition Catalogue*, translated by Stewart Spencer, 7. San Francisco: Chronicle Books, 1993.

———. Lecture at La Maison Française, New York University, 19 September 1995.

Index

Alquié, Ferdinand, 103
Angelique ou l'enchantement, 139
Anthropomorphism, 11
Auerbach, Erich, *Mimesis*, 9

Barthes, Roland, 10, 133
Barthelme, Donald, 13; postmodernism, 13, 14
Beckett, Samuel, 23; presence, 23; style, 23
Beautiful Captive, The (*La belle captive*), 117, 126
Bogue, Ronald, 131
Bousquet, Joë, 23, 107

Chateau, Dominique, 97
Creative process, 115; creator as modern artist, 125; creation from dream state, 126; creator exposed, 133–36; interpenetration of word and image, 117–21; problems of verbal/visual description, 46; uncertain narrator-creator, 128, 129, 132

Delvaux, Paul, 102, 104, 116, 131–32; chance in collage, 103; collage or assemblage, 102
Derniers jours de Corinthe, Les, 139
Description, 11, 24, 25, 77, 138–39; descriptive language as state of mind, 30–31; sound patterns of description, 38, 45, 51; spatial description, 38
Djinn, 98–101
Dream images, 28, 67, 82, 112, 114

Eagleton, Terry, 13
Editing, for change and movement, 113; for creating confusions and delusions, 70, 83; for fantasizing, 76; for imitating actions of the mind, 70; for special effects, 70; for states of mind, 76; for tempo and rhythm, 70; for transformations, 113
Erasers, The (*Les gommes*), 35, 35–58, 136

Fictional reality, 17, 24; false appearance of reality, 108; new reality, 25, 29, 35; new reality and new art, 55–56.
Film, 20; contamination principle, 29; phenomenological experience of film, 33; film as theater, 54
Flaubert, Gustave, 9, 17, 24, 25, 27
For a New Novel (*Pour un nouveau roman*), 10, 15, 21; "Elements of a Modern Anthology," 21; "Nature, Humanism, and Tragedy," 10; "New Novel, New Man," 146 n. 10
Foucault, Michel, 133
Fowlie, Wallace, 102–3
French new novel (nouveau roman), 11; Butor, Pinget, Duras, Simon, Ollier, Sarraute, 13; definition, 13

Generators, 26, 27; as inspiration, 87; motifs, 130–31; popular imagination, 61; popular myths as generators, 61
Ghosts in the Mirror (*Le miroir qui revient*), 15, 18, 139
"Graveyard of identities and Uniforms, A," 16; Henri de Corinthe, 16, 139

Hallucinations 18
Hamilton, David, 28, 102, 104, 131–32
Heath, Stephen, 10, 77
House of Assignation, The (*La maison de rendezvous*), 113

Imagination and vision, 25, 26, 126–27; labyrinthine confusions, 76–77; labyrinths of place, 87; routes, 26, 88–89
Immortal One, The (*L'immortelle*), 59–76, 113, 136
In the Labyrinth (*Dans le labyrinthe*), 59, 76–78
Iser, Wolfgang, 14, 57, 134; act of reading, 14, 18

Jameson, Frederic, 13–14
Jealousy (*La jalousie*), 59, 78–79
Jeu avec le feu, Le, 132

Kafka, Franz, 25

Langer, Susanne, 987
Language as *parole, langue, langage*, 20
Last Year at Marienbad (*L'année dernière à Marienbad*), 21, 59–60
Lippard, Lucy, 105
Ludic, 20
Lukacs, Georg, 19, 134

Magritte, René, 28, 102, 117–27
Man Who Lies, The (*L'homme qui ment*), 80–98, 136
Mazes and labyrinths, 18, 19, 35

Meaning, 11; slipping meaning, 33; stifled meaning, 25; verisimilitude, 25
Merleau-Ponty, Maurice, 10
Metamorphosis, 93; by description, 110; part of filmmaking process, 93; related to acting and lying, 94–96
Metonymy, 25; metaphor from generators, 25, 75, 121–23; metonymy as code, 123, 130; metonymy from personal sources, 121–23
Mise-en-abyme, as code, 123–24; as condensation of story, 86
Morrissette, Bruce, 12, 104; creative formalism, 12; recurring techniques in Robbe-Grillet, 12; values of art, 12

Narration, 80; child's play, 99; lying as a method of narrative structure, 870; shifting appearance of reality, 100; trial-and-error as fiction-making, 85
Narrators, 32; camera as narrator, 68–69; elusive narrator, 127; unobtrusive narrator, 77–78
Novel and film as theater, 54–55, 110, 127

Order and disorder, 33, 36–37, 41, 106

Parody and game playing, 47, 49–50, 58, 80, 98, 108
Patterns and motifs, 26, 116–17; creating narratives, 90
Perception, 10
Phenomenological thinking, 10, 11, 12, 86
Pinget, Robert, 24; elusive narrator, 24; style as movement, 24
Point of view, 30, 31, 54; erratic camera point of view, 83; obsession, 59, 70–76; perceptions as personal visions, 31
Progressive Slippages of Pleasure (*Glissements progressifs du plaisir*), 113, 132

INDEX

Project for a Revolution in New York (*Projet pour une revolution à New York*), 32

Rauschenberg, Robert, 104, 128, 131 32
Reading, 32; active reading, 32; communicative experience of reading, 134, 135; sensual experience of reading, 33, 38, 57
Realism, 9; real world, 12
Realist ideology, 17, 27, 31
Repetition, 76
Romanesques, 16; autobiographies, 25
Roussel, Raymond, 21

Sartre, Jean-Paul, 11
Shklovsky, Victor, 14
Siegel, Ronald, 18, 19
Sound and sensuality of text, 30; musical order of text, 63; sound themes, 83
Souvenirs du triangle d'or, 126
Spear, Thomas, 98
Storytelling, 18; narrative as experiment, 136; narrative diegesis, 19; rejecting expected narrative strategies, 18, 29
Sturrock, John, *The French New Novel*, 11–12

Subjective states of mind, 29; memory causing appearance of reality, 99; memory jolts, 29; time shifts in mind, 29
Sulieman, Susan, 31–32
Surrealism, 103, 137, 138; André Breton, 103
Svevo, Italo, 22–23

Tansey, Mark, 15–16
Time sequences, 29, 35, 36; evanescent nature of reality in time, 48; time as musical motives, 106; time as a generator, 37; time in memory, 38, 40, 67; time expressed in rhythm and movements, 44
Topology, 106; as properties of a mathematical figure, 106; as topography, 106
Tragedy, 11

Voice-over, 83; interrupted by contamination shots, 85; inventing story, 83
Voyeur, The (*Le voyeur*), 21, 113

Yarrow, Ralph, 98

OHIO UNIVERSITY LIBRARY

Please return this book as soon as you have finished with it. In order to avoid a fine it must be returned by the latest date stamped below. All books are subject to recall after two weeks or immediately if needed for reserve.

CF